THE TURNAROUND

THE TURNAROUND
FROM 0-10 TO 10-0

CHUCK MOTTLEY
WITH SANDRA B. GHOST

Jubilee Publishing   Scottsdale, Arizona

This special edition was prepared for printing by
Ghost River Images
5350 East Fourth Street
Tucson, Arizona 85711

Printed in the United States of America

First Printing: September, 1999

ISBN # 09674689-1-4

Library of Congress
99-96398
CIP

Contents

DEDICATION

This book is dedicated to Harry "Red" Caughron, my high school football coach, and to Louis "Weenie" Miller, my college basketball coach. Both of these men have served as lifelong patterning models for me. They showed me the delicately sensitive intricacies of leadership: how to motivate people; how to encourage others and extract the highest performance from them; how to overcome adversity; how to come from behind and win; how to maintain poise–and most important, how to apply these paradigms, learned in sports, to the game of life.

Red Caughron, who coached me at George Washington High School in Alexandria, Virginia, spent most of his coaching career at Woodberry Forest, a prep school in Virginia. His teams won 78% of their games, compiling a record for thirty-one years of 217 wins, 57 losses and 5 ties. The stellar teams he coached won 15 league titles in that time. He retired in 1992.

I had the opportunity to coach against Red for a couple of years. You can imagine the intimidating challenge which *that* presented.

Weenie Miller coached me in basketball at Hampden Sydney College in Virginia. I was his team captain. He later coached at VMI, where one of his teams won the Southern Conference Tournament and played in the NCAA Tournament. He finished his career as Athletic Director at Hampden Sydney College in 1992.

Years later, I realized the value of the power tools these two men had imparted, the molten principles which had been tucked into the pocket of my subconscious, to be taken out and applied when life presented adversity.

ACKNOWLEDGMENTS

There are many people to acknowledge and thank for their help with this endeavor. In fact, I frankly worry that I might leave someone out.

To my friends, who read the manuscript and offered suggestions: Tim Gay; Hal Mack; Gary Pryor; Dick Henderson; Chris Allen; and especially Jim Ricketts, who acted as my editor, a grateful "thank you" for your constructive comments.

To the Chaparral family–teachers, coaches, administrators, students, and to Andrea English, and Laurel Grider, who are always available and helpful to anyone who walks into the office at Chaparral High School–an all inclusive "thank you" for your support.

To the principal of Chaparral, John Kriekard, plus Jerry Dawson, the Athletic Director and all of the Varsity, Junior Varsity and Freshman Football Coaches–many thanks for your help and support.

To the women who helped with the typing, Janet Lyons and Carolyn Plotke, thank you for your diligence and patience in trying to decipher my handwriting.

To Penny Porter for lending her expertise and counsel, a grateful thank you; to Jane Estabrook and Jaime Waltman, much gratitude for your efforts in compiling game statistics and putting them into a booklet at the end of the year to be given to all the players at our banquet.

To Coni Monroe, for her faithfulness, wisdom and marketing expertise, much gratitude is due, and I am extremely grateful to Ron Christopher, and *THE TRIBUNE* newspaper for supplying photographs.

To my children, Josh, Jed, Douglass and Marcia, many thanks for your love and support; and to my wife, Linda, who is always positive and supportive: a very special thanks.

Needless to say, Ron Estabrook deserves an immense measure of gratitude for his commitment and high ideals, for without him there would have been no story to tell.

FOREWORD
By Coach Bruce Snyder,
Head Football Coach, A.S.U.

Wouldn't it be satisfying to look into a mirror at the end of a football season and say, "I gave all that I had to give!"

Coach Mottley has captured a moment in time when an outstanding coaching staff and a group of young men could say that they did just that! Chaparral's season was part magical, part hard work, and part genius.

So much hard work goes into a football season by all concerned. Tough decisions have to be made, wisdom as to when to push or to pull back at critical moments; hardships such as key injuries must be managed. This book is a must read for all parents of high school athletics, for administrators who need to see the value of successful athletics, and boosters who want to learn how to help while getting out of the way.

Simple and straightforward, Coach Mottley makes his point, supports it, and moves on. The lessons are here to be learned by coaches, administrators and boosters alike.

If you want to build a team, this book provides the blueprint.

INTRODUCTION

This is the remarkable story of a high school whose football team had never won a conference championship in 20 years. While its total athletic program had won the 4A Conference Arizona State Athletic Excellence Award for three straight years this had been accomplished without help from its poor football program.

In three years, however, it went from 0-10 to 10-0, and then this amazing transformation led the team into the State Playoffs. How did that happen? How *could* that happen? What game plan, what regimen, what psychology could possibly accomplish lighting such a blazing fire under the Firebirds football team? This is the story of what happppened at Chaparral High School in Scottsdale, Arizona in 1997, when a group of young warriors overcame many adverse conditions.

Today's society is a stark contradiction to the one in which the parents of the young men in the teams in *THE TURNAROUND* grew up. There is no required military service today for these young men to practice strict discipline, learn the value of commitment, self-denial, the rigid mental calisthenics of becoming a warrior.

Learning warrior-mentality does not necessarily apply only to those seeking careers in military service or law enforcement. It should be a set of principles to be richly employed to win with both feet planted on the highly competitive playing field of life. Managing a large corporation, starting one's own business, or making a living in one of the professions takes a mental toughness—a warrior mentality—which in turn, enables a husband and father to successfully care for his family.

One of the most satisfying things in my life has been to watch a tentative young man develop into a confident, tenacious young warrior. This is key to what coaches do: they encourage; they demand; they motivate; they help young men set goals and develop a sense of working together toward a common goal; they attempt to set the keystone in boys minds to build single individuals into a well-integrated team.

Coaching kids and helping them develop is my passion. Like any competitor I like to win, but there is something much more important than winning—preparing these young men for life. Accepting defeat with poise is just as important as displaying a winner's trophy. Honing attitudes and disciplines in young minds is what this book is all about. The excitement these pages contain can be accomplished in any sport, in any school, if the proper power tools are connected to the power source...

Chuck Mottley
July, 1999

CHAPTER ONE

"JUST ONE MORE GAME"

Fading scarlet ribbons of sunset, laced with puffy gray widening jet trails, haloed the western skyline. John Kriekard, principal of Chaparral High School and his wife, Janie, drove down from their home on the McDowell mountains. He maintained the speed limit, but pushed a bit to get to the Chaparral game with Mingus High School. He always stood in the same spot every game, home or away—about 20 yards to the left of the Chaparral bench. One more victory in this semi-final game and Chaparral would be playing in the 4-A Championship game at Arizona State University's Sun Devil Stadium. He sure would like to be standing in his usual position *there.*

The Friday night air was crisp. John rolled up the car windows. It was Thanksgiving weekend, November 28th—ASU was playing U of A. He turned on the car radio and scrolled past a jumble of voices to pick up their game. His feelings tumbled over each other: excitement over Chaparral's game tonight; frustration over the fact that U of A was beating ASU.

The edges of his moustache dipped downward as he frowned at yardage lost by ASU in the play. "I just hope the Firebirds hold their own tonight better than ASU." He turned the volume down a notch.

11

Janie patted her husband's shoulder. "Honey, even if the Firebirds don't win, they've fulfilled your theme of the 'Tradition of Excellence'. In the three years you've been at Chaparral you've instilled that vision in the students in both academics and athletics. What more could you want?"

"An undefeated football season." He smiled and the mustache formed its usual broad slash.

His thoughts overrode the excited voice of the radio announcer. His theme of "Excellence" had been well received by parents, students and faculty. Janie was right, the school had risen to those goals. He had to admit to himself though, that he had been less than confident about the Firebirds football team. He frankly didn't believe that a suburban, affluent, high school of over 1700 in enrollment could get young men to discipline themselves over their four years in high school football.

The car headlights briefly illuminated a small field of tall cactus standing at attention like bristling sentinels. He turned on the car heater. The action precipitated another thought: *It was really instituting the weight training program which turned up the heat on the team. I swear I just didn't believe that Ron Estabrook could pull it off–make them weight train all year long–didn't think they could be that self-disciplined.*

Ron's been the catalyst to light a fire under the Firebirds. This team has really surprised, no...shocked me...it's been one of my most satisfying career experiences watching this year's spirited team. Only two negatives–the injury to Jerry's knee, and the continuing Johnson problem.

He turned into the approach to Shadow Mountain High School, the neutral site of this semi-final playoff game. A slow line of cars inched forward to the parking lot. *Growing up in a rural community,* John thought, *I know just how fired up a rural team can get when they play a more affluent, suburban school...that's the way it always is when Mingus plays Chaparral–it's so tough.* He down-shifted and inched forward a few more feet. *Jerry's the key to a state championship,* he told himself. *I wonder how his knee will hold up in this game. If he can just get through this one, he'll have two more weeks of rehabilitation.*

He snapped off the radio as frustration mounted higher at the ASU vs U of A game. "You know, Janie, you're right. I've always believed interscholastic events are instrumental to building well-rounded students. Even if the Firebirds don't win tonight, they have still fulfilled all the criteria of the Tradition of Excellence." He maneuvered the car into a space behind a tan Ford Explorer. Cheerleaders inside the car waved scarlet and gold pom-poms in time to the Firebird's fight song, sung at ear-splitting volume.

Janie smiled broadly. "So... win, lose, or draw, they've had a tremendous season, right?"

"Right!" he winced slightly at her incisive extraction of this admission. "But I sure would like to see an undefeated record," he grinned. "Just one more game," he whispered under his breath.

•   •   •

Sam and Kim Schwartzberg left earlier than usual for the 7:00 PM game that Friday night. Shadow Mountain High School was just five minutes away from their home, but they wanted to arrive at least 30 minutes before game-time to watch Jerry go through his pre-game warm-up. Their son had been injured in a freak accident during the seventh game of the year–the Apache Junction game, and now, this would just be his second game since the terrible misfortune. They wanted to assess how restrictive the huge brace on his right knee was–watch him run.

Jerry was 6', 200 pounds and ran the 40 in 4.5–a handsome young man whose eyes could suddenly change into rivets of steel, transformed by bold determination. He had been the starting fullback since his sophomore year, was second team All-State his junior year, and had broken most of the school's rushing records.

Until the Apache Junction game, he had been averaging over 200 yards rushing per game, and everyone anticipated he would be named Arizona's "Player of the Year." Division I colleges were calling every week. It appeared Jerry would have a wide choice of colleges to pick from...until the tragic accident. The phone now became silent–college coaches stopped calling.

It seemed so unfair. He had literally become a self-made athlete because of his driving hard work and dedication: an inspiration to his teammates; a role model for underclassmen; a young man everyone admired and respected.

As Sam and Kim rode quietly to the game, each immersed in their own thoughts, Kim wondered, *Why Jerry? Why him? Life can be so unfair. He doesn't deserve this when he's worked so hard...*

She bit her lip and looked out the car window as they neared Shadow Mountain. Since the accident it was like watching a beautiful, wild stallion be confined to a small fenced area where he was forced to walk slowly in a circle. Once the telephone had stopped ringing, Kim worried that the fabric of their son's life had been torn–not just the ligament in his right knee.

Sam parked the car and they hurried toward the field to watch the pre-game warm-up. They were both still hopeful Jerry would realize his dream of playing in the State Championship game at Sun Devil Stadium. "Just one more game," Sam said as he squeezed her hand.

•   •   •

This was not an entirely new experience for Alan and Irene Goodworth. Two years earlier their oldest son, who played defensive end at Saguaro High School, had played in the State Championship game at Sun Devil Stadium. Saguaro had won.

Scottsdale permits a crossover election of schools by choice. Now they hoped their younger son, Adam, might have the same opportunity playing for Chaparral. Adam was All-Conference, All-City tight end and had been first string since his sophomore year. They were proud of both their sons and marveled at what a multi-faceted person their younger son had become.

"Goody" was 6'2", 215 pounds, with large adroit hands which caught every pass thrown in his direction. Adam was also an outstanding blocker at his tight end position. His goatee and blond pony tail somehow gave him the look of a Biblical prophet–especially when he led the team in prayer and Bible study after the Thursday afternoon practices–until he roared out of the parking lot to go home on his Harley motorcycle.

If some marched to the beat of a different drummer, Adam Goodworth seemed to have the entire band orchestrating his free-spirited steps in life. In addition to being gifted in other areas, he was also an Honor student with a 4.0 plus grade point average.

Alan and Irene Goodworth had every reason to be extremely proud, and to hope they would have the unusual experience of watching both of their sons play in a State Championship game for two different teams. Just one more game, and then they'd know if that experience would be available to them.

• • •

Cyndie Muschinski was lost in her own thoughts as she drove to the game that night. How she wished that Clay's father could be here to see him play! It had not been easy raising Clay and his older brother Corbin, after their father's death. She was thankful, however, that Clay had strong men in his life, like the football coaches at Chapparal.

She was relieved that the early summer confrontation between Clay and Coach Estabrook had been quickly resolved. Coach Estabrook had insisted on Clay's commitment to the weight training program. The discipline had paid off–Clay's coaches were telling her he was one of the best offensive linemen in the State of Arizona.

She was so proud of her son; his round face with mischievous eyes surprisingly transformed into "eyes of the tiger" on the field. As a sophomore, he had made the All-Conference team on both the offense and defensive line. Even though Clay was 6'2",

260 pounds, he was considered small for Division I colleges, but Cyndie knew there would be many college scouts at the State Championship game to see her son play. Just one more game...

She knew in her heart her husband that would be watching.

• • •

As Jennifer Way opened the door of the brown pickup truck in their driveway that Friday night and settled into the passenger seat, she turned to her husband Ron, "Well, no more snack bar duty," she said with a touch of remorse. After four years, she was going to miss it all: being on the Booster Club; running the Snack Bar at the freshman, junior varsity and varsity football games; ordering food; organizing other parent's duties. She would particularly miss working with Kim Schwartzberg these four years. All the time and effort had been well worth it–she considered it had been a rare gift to be allowed to watch these gangly, uncoordinated young boys grow into confident, athletically skilled young men over the past four years.

Ron and Jennifer's son, Matt, had been first string as a sophomore and was good enough to make All-City as an offensive lineman that year. Then, in his junior year, he seemed to have lost enthusiasm for football; however, this year had been a vastly different story. Matt, who was 6'1", lost 40 pounds and trimmed down to 190 pounds. He was elected one of the team's co-captains, changed positions to linebacker and was now considered to be the best linebacker in the Conference.

The Ways never knew exactly what had happened in their son's junior year, nor did the coaches. Matt had the admirable quality of a very direct look, but the eyes and handsome face revealed nothing. There was no way to ascertain what he was thinking. And while his interest lost momentum during that one year, the Ways knew their son was now having fun, which was reflected in his performing well this year. Just one more game until Sun Devil Stadium. Ron and Jennifer would keep their fingers crossed.

•   •   •

Jacob ("Jake") Ireland was a co-captain, had made All-Conference at both offensive guard and linebacker. He had blocked two field goals which had saved victories. He had blocked a punt in the playoff game with Saguaro– the catalyst which had gotten the momentum going in the right direction.

He announced his individuality by changing hair color and styles, not quite as outrageously as Dennis Rodman, but somehow it seemed to dominate the topic of conversation in meetings.

When his best friend, Jerry Schwartzberg, had been injured in the Apache Junction game, their bond was so tightly cohesive that Jake had even felt his fallen teammate's pain in the training room. The picture of Jerry lying helpless on the ground still lingered with him. Even though Jerry had returned and played in the first two playoff games, he could discern this wasn't the same Jerry who had begun the season.

Now, the night of the game with Mingus at Shadow Mountain, Jake walked down the aisle of the team bus. He was a rock solid 5'10", 205 pounds. Jerry followed him down the aisle. Jake took the inside seat so that his best friend's right leg could extend into the aisle. He looked out the window as memories with Jerry began to reel across the screen of his subconscious.

We've come a long way together this past year...we've been inseparable...worked out every day, even Sundays, until our parents jumped on us about it and made us stop. "Take just one day off, one day of rest," he remembered them saying. *We put our parents through a lot, but all the hard work paid off—we were having an awesome year until Jerry's accident.* He thought back to all the stadiums the two of them had visited at night in July to get "the feel" of opposing team's fields.

Jake's father, Dan, never missed a game when Jake played, and his mother, Joell, was vigorously active on the Booster Club. Now, as the team traveled to Shadow Mountain High School, Jake tried to focus, to concentrate on the good times they had experienced. He tried to keep from thinking about Jerry's knee...tried to sift out any troubling doubts that Jerry might not hold up. *If we can just keep our former momentum, keep our drive in high gear for one more game, we'll make it to the Sun Devil Stadium. Hold it together for one more game, guys...*

• • •

As the school bus carrying the Chaparral football team pulled out of the parking lot, Coach Estabrook stood, as was his custom, and looked toward the rear of the bus. He always made sure all his players were seated. The driver shifted into second gear and Ron steadied himself momentarily before sitting down. Restrained excitement swirled around the players, as the bus roared into third gear–they were on their way.

Ron Estabrook soon became lost in his own thoughts, *Is this game plan going to work? We should be able to beat these guys... we're really thin with Jerry running less than full speed and Johnson's ankle at about 60%..Larry Zak won't start... so we're going with an inexperienced junior at corner back.* He grimaced with the intensity of the thoughts, and adjusted the position of his tinted glasses with one finger. *We're sure beat up, but we've always risen to the occasion before.*

He wanted vindication for what had happened in the 1996 season, not just for himself and his program, but for Chaparral. He thought back to 1995 and the season which was his first year as Head Coach. Chaparral had surprised everyone by winning six games and losing four, coming off a 0 - 10 year. The Firebirds had won the Conference Championship for the first time in its 20 year history–what a tremendous victory that had been in itself! They had gone to the Playoffs, and although they lost in the first round to Cactus, 38 to 24, the season was a huge success.

The Arizona Republic had selected Ron the 4-A "Coach of the Year," but the momentum of that 1995 year did not carry over to the 1996 season. There had been high expectations for the team in 1996, but it was like watching the air slowly go out of a football. It had been a deflating experience for Ron too. The season ended with a 5 and 5 record.

His thoughts returned to that season. *The kids just weren't ready for success and didn't have the intensity needed to win the big one. We lost four games by 8 or less points. All four of those teams went to the playoffs, and one of those, Tempe, won the State Championship.*

Although Ron felt that he had coached harder in 1996, that team never seemed to reach the goals and level of play that they were capable of reaching. It was only his second year at Chaparral, but in all his years of coaching high school football, he had never had a year like that one. It left a bitter taste in his mouth. It all lay in the fortitude of total commitment, and as he plumbed the depth of his own, his assistant coaches and players, it was found lacking.

The 1996 team was expected to make the Playoffs, and after the last game, a loss to Gilbert, 35-7, he called the team together in the end zone, underneath the scoreboard. He now remembered that moment very well—it was actually the genesis of the 1997 season—the birth of a new dedication.

He thanked the seniors for their contribution to the team and dismissed them. Then, to the remaining juniors and one sophomore he announced, "This season is over tonight. But tonight, right now, we are starting next season." Several eyes widened. "On Monday, we start our weight program. I want a commitment from each one of you right now for next season. Are you committed?"

With one voice they pledged a loud "Yes sir!" It would have made an army drill sergeant proud.

Ron had made up his mind that unless a player participated in the off-season weight program, they would not play on the varsity, no exceptions. They could play football on the JV team without working in the weight program, but not on the Varsity team. There had been too many players on the '96 team who did not make the necessary commitment and the whole team had paid for it. It had penalized those who did work out diligently, ultimately hindering the entire program. "Mixed commitment does not make a team," he would tell his players and coaches.

The following week, Darren Urban, the high school sports writer for The Tribune wrote a column with the headline, "Miscues Cost Firebirds." He summarized the year for the six high schools in Scottsdale. His column told about Chaparral's disappointing season and questioned whether the football program had really turned the corner as had been thought in 1995. Ron knew that this definitely did not evidence Dr. Kriekard's idea of a "Tradition of Excellence."

He copied the newspaper column and tacked it on the bulletin board beside his desk in the football coaching office. It was in a predominant place where he could see it every day. There were several sentences he highlighted in yellow, and it served to keep him rigidly motivated–unyieldingly focused.

This year had not been easy. He had expended more time on the football program than he had intended. His insurance business suffered because of it, but he really felt he had no choice. Demanding a deeper commitment from his players and coaches, as their leader he couldn't short change his own.

As he reflected, he knew there were times when he got close to the line in his obsessive drive to have all of his players and coaches reach their highest potential. Justification for such a demanding approach soon came in the improvement they displayed.

Ron believed that you get what you demand from both players and coaches. His goal was to put them into a position to be successful, to set a high standard–demand excellence; however the goals must be attainable. If they are not, then you may be responsible for creating unfair expectations.

He was pleased with what had happened this year–the way in which the community, the school, players and coaches had all come together. There were only two dark clouds: Jerry's injury; and the problem with Scott Johnson's father. The expectations had not been set too high. The apathy around the football program that he had inherited, had been transformed into excited commitment. All the slogans, all the T-shirts with "no Fear" and "War" were now worn with pride by everyone associated with the Chaparral foot-ball program.

He turned from the window...and his thoughts. As he glanced around the bus he was filled with pride in this group of young men, particularly the players who had come up from the JV team as freshmen and started as sophomores: Schwartzberg; Johnson; Way; Goodworth and Muschinski. He turned around in his seat and faced me, "Chuck, first Mingus–need to take care of business tonight–one more game, and then on to Sun Devil Stadium."

•   •   •

His statement abruptly brought me out of a cocoon of my own thoughts as I sat in my usual seat on the bus behind him. I had been at Chaparral before Ron had arrived; first, in the role of father; and then, as an assistant coach.

My son, Jed, played wide receiver and cornerback on the JV team for a year, and then on the Varsity team for two years. After Jed graduated, I was asked by Gary Mauldin, who had just been hired as the new football coach in 1994, if I would be interested in being an assistant coach the following year. My business situation allowed me enough time to help out, so I accepted.

The year turned out to be a galloping disaster. There were only two seniors returning who had ever played in a Varsity foot-ball game. Then, to compound this calamity, fifteen kids were lost for the year due to injuries, and they had all been starters. They had only a couple of close games, as Chaparral became the league whipping boy going 0 - 10. I remember predicting it would take three years to turn the program around–I just had no idea it would start so badly.

This season, 1997, had been an important year for me per-sonally–a vindication, but in a different sense than Ron Estabrook's vindication. I needed to unpack the chip on my shoulder from that 0 - 10 season–it was a stigma I desperately wanted to over-come.

Also, there was another vindication. Ron was my friend, and it hurt when I heard the barbs that Chuck Johnson, the father of our quarterback, had aimed at Ron and our program. His slams were verbalized before the season had started, during a 4 on 4 passing game. He announced to me, "Estabrook is a 5 and 5 coach, at best 6 and 4." I never told Ron what he had said, but the words stung me personally.

As the bus driver downshifted, I struggled to make a legible note in my journal which I had kept for the past four years. I had vowed that if we went to the State Championship, I would write a book about what had happened here at Chaparral High School to go from 0 - 10 to 10 - 0. Tonight, I silently renewed that pledge. The strategies, the communication, the programs, the psychology could serve as paradigms to lift other teams to climb their own Mount Everest. But we had to get this semi-final behind us first— just one more game!

CHAPTER TWO

"THE CATALYST"

Who was responsible for so dramatically turning this football program around at Chaparral High School?

Physically, he was 5' 11", 190 pounds, an attractive man in his mid-fifties who had stayed in shape, conscientiously making sure his waist had maintained a size 34. He had worn a mustache for some years now. His face had the rugged, craggy look which spoke of exposure to the sun's rays, a badge worn by coaches who are in the sun for four or five months a year–especially in the 6,200 ft. elevation of the Lake Tahoe area.

Ron Estabrook had been the head football coach for five years at Truckee High School, which was located about 15 miles northeast of Lake Tahoe, and about 30 miles west of Reno, Nevada. Even though Truckee was in California in the Sierras, it was so far away from other California high schools, that it was only logical and feasible to play in the Nevada Double A league.

His football playing experience consisted of playing offensive guard in high school and defensive end in college. During his head coaching tenure at Truckee from 1989 to 1993, the team compiled a record of 50 wins and just 7 losses in those five years. They reached the Playoffs every year–winning the State Championship twice.

When Ron first moved to Truckee, he started an insurance agency there and became active in the community. He was the leader in starting the Pop Warner football program, and with four extremely athletic sons, he found himself investing many hours coaching Little League baseball and also coached Pop Warner for eighteen years.

Two months before the Truckee High School football season began in 1986, the Junior Varsity coach became ill. Ron was asked to coach the JV team and in his three years as head JV coach, his teams had 24 wins and 3 losses.

It was a curious enigma that even though Ron had known success at every level of his coaching experience, he had suffered through his first three years of Pop Warner winning only one game. Those three years, however, molded coaching skills and fine-tuned his rare abilities. He coached for love of the game and the kids. Every year the program grew by one team, because the kids learned football and had fun–the two most important ingredients in coaching. It was through this period he began to refine the steps it took to build a solid program; he learned the art of teaching the fundamentals of the game, while maintaining the sensitive balance between encouragement and discipline. He discovered there was a way to get parents involved–a factor absolutely essential to fostering a vigorous football program and cooperative environment.

These elements began to solidify into results. In the following three years, out of six Pop Warner teams, three had State Championships in Northern California.

Coach Estabrook's natural gifts of administration and organization, which he utilized so well in business, plus his exceptional ability to communicate skillfully, helped seed an athletic program in Truckee which bore harvest a few years later when he was asked to become the head coach at Truckee High School in 1989.

Things began to come full circle. The same kids he had coached in Pop Warner were now his Varsity football players. In the past twenty years the school record for the best year was 7 wins and 2 losses in 1982. In 1990 and 1993, Truckee won the

Nevada Double A State Championship, and Ron captured Nevada Coach of the Year honors both years.

The 1993 team would be his last as he and his wife, Jane, were tired of the cold winters of Lake Tahoe. They longed for the sun and warmth of Scottsdale, Arizona after years of dealing with thigh-high snow storms, and icicles the size of stalactites in Mammoth cave hanging from their guttering. Ron resigned as coach, sold his insurance agency and moved his family to Arizona. Little did he know, at the time, how unforeseen events were lining up to utilize his talents in the "valley of the sun."

An artist acquaintance of the Estabrooks from Truckee had also moved to Scottsdale at about the same time in August of 1994. While enrolling her child at Chaparral High School, she was told by one of the secretaries that Chaparral did not have a very good football program.

She responded, "Well, you have a very successful high school coach who has moved to the area. Why don't you call him and see if he would be interested in helping?" She wrote Ron's home telephone number down, and handed it to the woman.

The secretary called Gary Mauldin, the newly hired Chaparral football coach, and gave him the phone number. Gary called Ron immediately asking if he would be interested in being a varsity assistant coach. Ron wasn't sure he would have the amount of time available that the varsity team would require—he was in the process of getting his new insurance career off and running. After further conversation, he learned the junior varsity head coaching job was not filled. He offered to take that job and help on Friday nights at varsity games. Gary Mauldin eagerly accepted his proposition.

And so, through a random conversation between a secretary at Chaparral and a transfer student's parent, the wheels were set in motion for the transformation of Chaparral football.

While the Chaparral varsity lost all of their games, going 0 - 10, in 1994, the junior varsity won 4, lost 3, and tied 1. Ron did not have enough players on his JV team. Normally the team is made up of sophomores, with perhaps two or three juniors who were not ready to play for the varsity. He brought up 7 freshmen

25

to the JV team, which was an adventuresome and innovative solution.

Five of those seven freshmen: Scott Johnson; Jerry Schwarzberg; Matt Way; Adam Goodworth and Clay Muschinski moved up to the varsity team the following year as sophomores. The other two, David Williams and Chris Dobbins, played another year with the JV.

After the football season was over, Gary Mauldin again asked Ron to join the varsity staff–this time as offensive coordinator. Ron took some time to talk it over with his wife and the parents of some of the JV students who wanted him to move up to the varsity team with their sons.

Calls also began to come from varsity parents encouraging him to help out at the varsity level. It was obvious that his kids on the JV team were not only focused, but they were having fun as well.

Coach Estabrook firmly believed getting his team into a serious weight lifting program was key, and if the inadequate facilities and equipment could be improved, it would be the springboard to develop a quality football program. He had become extremely attached to the players, as coaches are prone to do, and had the vision to discern their qualities deserving of development. He made the decision to help coach at the varsity level the next year.

That first spring practice, which started the first week of May and ran for three weeks, was used to install Ron's Wing T formation, which he had employed so successfully at Truckee. And then the last week in May, the Summer Passing League (seven against seven playing touch football) started. Chaparral played about 12 - 15 games against local high school teams, such as Horizon, Paradise Valley, Arcadia, North Canyon, and Saguaro.

Also scheduled was a Passing League Tournament at San Diego State University on June 16 and 17th, 1995. The day before the team was to leave for San Diego, Head Coach Gary Mauldin resigned. He admitted he was "burned out" and had decided to take off the next year, then attempt to re-enter coaching the following year.

Ron took the team to the San Diego Tournament. The team won four games–lost three. The passing game had definitely improved from the previous year. The kids felt good about themselves and had every reason to let their self-esteem take wing. They had beaten two of the top teams in Southern California.

A brief incident at the tournament seemed to herald the fact that the team had reached a true turning point in their football program. A San Diego State University assistant coach came up to one of the Chaparral coaches after a particular game and said, "Who are you guys? Do you know whom you just beat?" That remark inflated their chest measurements for the day! However, it was really the first significant reinforcement that there had been a turnaround.

The 25 football players and many parents who went to San Diego, in addition to the assistant coaches, all expected Ron Estabrook to be named the new head coach. There was only one problem–the new principal, John Kriekard, had just started his job, and at the time knew nothing about the depth of Ron's background. All he knew was that his football coach had resigned, so he "posted" the job, which meant the specifications and requirements were displayed on the bulletin board at Chapparal. In addition, the opening was circulated throughout the Scottsdale School District.

John Kriekard had been a former middle school principal and assistant superintendent in the Scottsdale School District. Hiring a new football coach was a major decision to face in his first week of a new position.

Dr. Kriekard earnestly wanted to make the right decision, but having been in the school system in other capacities, he was also aware of the politics involved in such a decision. Propriety seemed to dictate that as there were four former head coaches on staff, who were presently teaching, they should be approached first. All four declined any interest in applying for the position.

John Kriekard then began calling friends and acquaintances in the Scottsdale and Paradise Valley School Districts for recommendations. He felt it was important to have a coach who would be on campus full-time as a teacher. He had met Ron Estabrook one time, but felt it was in the best interest of the school not to have a businessman and off-campus coach be the next head coach at Chaparral High School. He was later to reverse that thinking when acquainted with the outstanding accomplishments woven into the fabric of Ron's record.

One name kept surfacing in John's search: an assistant football coach at one of the Paradise Valley District Schools. After receiving a list of references from the prospective coach, John began calling those references–they were lukewarm, which surprised him.

In the meantime, John was visited by Chuck Johnson, the father of two players, both quarterbacks–one who played on the JV team the year prior, Scott, and his older brother, Brian. Brian had played quarterback on the 0 - 10 team. Chuck Johnson recommended that the new principal hire Ron Estabrook. Ron was convinced by several parents to put his application in, which he did three days before the interview.

John Kriekard then decided to interview both candidates, the assistant from the Paradise Valley District and Ron Estabrook. He planned to invite the Athletic Director, Jerry Dawson, who was also the baseball coach. In twenty-four years, Jerry had completed 449 wins and 230 losses with one State championship. He was considered the "Dean" of baseball coaches in the State. Also invited was the President of the Booster Club, Rudy Miller, to be present at the meeting. Miller was a strong Estabrook supporter. His son, Rod, had played on the JV team. He remembered how the kids seemed to have fun while still working hard; the successful balance between discipline and encouragement their coach maintained.

Ron Estabrook was the second candidate interviewed. After he left, John turned to Rudy and Jerry, he smiled broadly, "As far as I'm concerned, Ron blew him away. There's no comparison between the two." The others nodded in agreement.

Ron made a commitment to Dr. Kriekard to be part of the day-to-day activities: to monitor grades, and to be available to them after school, before practice began. He diligently honored this commitment. If a team member got in trouble with the school, an administrator would immediately call Ron at his insurance office. Because of his availability, the team really was not aware that he was an "off campus" coach.

John left the interview meeting and walked down the hall to the conference room where eight of the senior football players had assembled. There was an obvious air of tension as he entered the room. They all realized that this decision would impact their performance for the season, and Chaparral's future football standings.

Dr. Kriekard raised one hand as though to signal "quiet," but it was actually unnecessary. The room had fallen silent.

"I want to hear your comments," he told them, "but first, I want to announce that Ron Estabrook is the new head football coach at Chaparral High School."

The room erupted in cheers and applause. Statistic's don't lie, and Ron Estabrook had seemed to tap into just the right formula to produce those statistics. Little did any of them know that day that the kindling had just been set in place which would light a fire under the Firebirds–Coach Estabrook had the torch smoldering in his pocket...

CHAPTER THREE

"THE GOOD, THE BAD AND THE UGLY"

In late December, 1996, Coach Estabrook wrote a letter to all prospective football players at Chaparral High School, and included the following quote:

Vince Lombardi said, "To me football is more than diagrams and techniques. It is a lot like life in demanding a man's personal commitment to excellence and to victory. But to achieve success, whatever the job we have, we must pay the price for success. It's like anything worthwhile, IT HAS A PRICE. You have to pay the price to win, and you have to pay the price to get to the point where success is possible. <u>Most important, you must pay the price to stay there.</u> Success is not a 'sometimes thing.' In other words, you don't do what is right once in awhile, but all the time. Success is a habit. Winning is a habit...unfortunately, so is losing."

Also included in this same letter, was the announcement that weight lifting would start Monday, January 6th, 1997.

Granted, this proclamation was met with a few moans and groans at the time, but it was a bugle sounding reveille. It was a wake up call to the disciplines and commitments which would lead the team to an undefeated season.

Throughout the months of spring, while desert cactus bloomed, sporting bouquets of flowers like jaunty Easter bonnets atop their heads, the team pumped iron. Throughout the months of summer they sweated like punctured garden hoses. They sacrificed movies, dates, and computer games to bite on the bullet of self-discipline. They grew stronger, "learned their jobs," according to Ron.

Their dance card for the entire season was an eye-crossing schedule of the toughest opponents in the state. Five of the first six teams to be played were ranked in the top ten of Class 4A. They were going to need all the help they could get for their first game of the season with Cactus high school. When you dance with a cactus it can be a prickly and dangerous encounter.

•   •   •

Football coaches live within the parameters of a rigid bottom-line reality–their teams either win or lose–black or white, no subtle shadings of gray. A loss is the consequential payback for mistakes made, both mental and physical. Not to say they go home after a loss, kick the cat and forget to kiss their wives goodnight; however, they are haunted by the fallout of things left undone in team preparation the week before the game. Those miscalculations jump over the goalposts of their subconscious, in tandem with sheep counted, while trying to go to sleep that night. The competition which results in winning or losing is heartlessly unforgiving to the losers.

As the first game of the season with Cactus high school approached, the coaches plotted like generals in the Pentagon–it was war. Even though Chaparral was ranked number 3 by Barry Sollenberg in his *ARIZONA FOOTBALL MAGAZINE* in the pre-season polls, this was the real world. All that counted was where we would end up in power points as five of our first six opponents were ranked in the Top Ten. The scheduling could have caused coronaries of intimidation, but the coaches emphasized repeatedly, "Look, we're going to have to play these teams in the playoffs, playing them now in the regular season can only help us." And it did.

In an unusual quirk of scheduling, six of the 46 teams in 4A started the season one week early. Cactus was one of those teams, which gave us a burly "leg up" in using this opportunity to scout their game against Moon Valley. Not only did the coaches attend, but we encouraged the team to scout their game. Most did.

The following Saturday morning, we swung into high gear. At 8:00 AM the coaching staff watched a film of a scrimmage with Glendale High School played on the Thursday night prior to scouting the Cactus game on Friday. Each coach graded his position players, and then at 10:00 AM the kids convened. We put them through paces of some light running on the field, and a light workout in the weight room. At 10:45 AM, the team gathered in the meeting room to watch the film.

Around noon, the kids left, and then the real work began for the coaches as we watched and "broke down" the other team's defense and offense of their previous games. It was customary to exchange the previous three game films with the upcoming opponent; however, that wasn't possible this early in the season. Since we hadn't played a game yet, we exchanged film of our scrimmage with Glendale–they traded us their scrimmage game vs Bradshaw Mountain.

The scouting reports of the actual Cactus game, however, were like sending a U-2 surveillance plane over Iraq. The information gleaned allowed us to chart their offensive plays and snap an abbreviated satellite photo of tendencies their offense preferred. That information was fed into the computer, which gave us printouts of formations run, plays run, and on what down they liked to run those plays. The war room chess game began.

Dana Zupke, our defensive coordinator, Scott Heideman, offensive line and linebackers coach, and I, huddled over our printouts after watching film of their scrimmage. My coaching of cornerbacks and involvement as special teams coordinator dictated an intense concern about Cactus' passing game. They had a long history of having one of the State's best. Larry Fetkenhier, Cactus head coach, had gained a formidable reputation for developing quarterbacks, and Beasley, his quarterback of two years prior, had set a number of State passing records–he was now playing for Kansas State.

I studied their pass patterns carefully and laid the computer printout aside. "Even though their quarterback is a sophomore, I sure was impressed on his play action faking, then on his rollout. He gets a lot of depth... gives him time to throw long."

Dana and Scott both nodded in agreement.

"I'm worried about that," I told them. "How do we contain him? That slash pattern is dangerous." (The slash pattern is when a wide receiver will run straight down the field for 8 - 10 yards, cut to the inside for a few steps and then change direction 180 degrees and run toward the sidelines.)

Dana smiled, stroking his small goatee thoughtfully. "I agree, we've got to contain him, but I think we've got to stop the run first. Let's make their sophomore quarterback beat us."

I ran a hand over my own face, felt a bristly stubble sprouting in the heat of early afternoon and wished I'd taken time to shave. "Yeah, you're right. We'll concentrate on that slash pattern in our group drills this week."

Dana removed the cap from a small bottle of Evian water on the table by his printout. He took a large swig before telling us, "My chief concern is their running game. Their two backs are as big as we'll see this year. Their tailback has good speed, he's 6'1", 190 pounds, and that fullback is about 225 pounds. He's a first rate blocker."

Scott riffled through the pages of his printout, "The kid's a great blocker," he added.

Dana continued his assessment. "Look, with our offense, we're going to score a lot of points. The downside is they've got a huge offensive line, probably outweigh us 30 to 40 pounds per man. It's the Great Wall of China against a picket fence by comparison, but if we can just hold them to three TD's, we should beat them."

Ron Estabrook was also the offensive coordinator. He and Jim Ellison, the JV coach, had their own huddle going in the players' meeting room, armed with their Cactus scrimmage and scouting notes. They weren't sure whether Cactus would run their 4-3 defense against us, or their 5-3. Two years prior, we had played Cactus in their first playoff game. We played them even for the first three quarters, but they put the game away in the last quarter as Beasley and their big line just plain wore us down. In that game, Cactus, who had been using a 4-3 all year, came out in a 5-3, but our offense moved the ball so well on them early in the game, they switched back to their 4-3.

To the casual observer of football games, whether a team uses a 4-3 or 5-3 probably doesn't make much difference, but to an offensive coordinator and the offensive line coach it is extremely critical. When a defense uses a 5-3, and puts a defensive nose guard over the center, it changes the blocking assignments. It is important particularly in a wing T offense, which pulls its guards on almost every play. (We use a tackle trap and misdirection plays to throw off the defensive linebackers if they try to key on the guards.)

Once Ron and Jim finished with their analysis, they joined us in the coaches' office. It would now be time to integrate strategy, plot the game plan for the coming Cactus game. Ron held an Italian sub sandwich with one hand, picked up a thick piece of chalk with the other, and began diagraming on the blackboard just how he thought their defense would line up against each of our five formations. (See Appendix II) He diligently went over every play from each of our five formations, and blocked it with every offensive blocker to make sure that the play would work against that particular defense. This was his signature methodology employed each week of the season. This eliminated plays and formations that were marginal against their defensive sets.

Next, he outlined special plays we would use that week–plays which would attack specific weaknesses of that particular defense. Subsequently the pass patterns were drawn up, the drop back patterns, and the play action patterns which would attack the upcoming opponent's defense.

He always encouraged all of the assistant coaches to contribute their thoughts and suggestions. Differences of opinion sometimes led to crisp, but healthy disagreements; however, by late

Saturday afternoon we always had a significant consensus of the battle plan.

That Saturday, at about 4:30 PM, Ron leaned against the blackboard. He cleaned chalk dust off his tinted glasses and told us, "They're big up front, but I think we can trap them, run the belly, and run outside. The defensive backs are small. If we can break Jerry into the open field, they're going to have a hard time tackling him. He's just too strong–he'll break tackles."

I was responsible each week for the special team's game plan. I usually took film home to watch on Sunday. Ron and Dana did likewise. I had kept a log on all our opponents. The first thing I did on Sunday was go back to 1996, when we played Cactus in the playoffs. Some surprises presented themselves. As a result of this review, I sent the following fax to Ron:

"Re: Cactus9/1/97

Ron:

I think that we need to make teams pay if they gamble or do things on special teams such as Cactus:

1) Putting four men together on their 25 yard line on kick offs and challenging you to pooch or onside;

2) Rushing on punt blocks and leaving no one to protect on sweep, or pass to RE; they also leave a hole to the left of our center. We could run the fake punt there;

3) On XP, rushing 9 or 10 men leaving 2 point conversion open.

I recommend that we take away their aggressiveness the first chance that we can–it will slow them up for the rest of the game."

And so, the next week we worked on pooch kick offs (instead of kicking off deep, to "pooch kick" means to kick it only 25-30 yards in the air behind their 5 linemen who are lined up on the 50. This puts it in front of their blockers, who are lined up on the 25 yard line prepared to form a wedge for the deep receivers who would normally catch the kicked ball.)

We also put emphasis on the fake punt. Our guys drilled on this play. In punt formation the center snaps the ball to the protector, who lines up 5 yards from center and is positioned to block the first man who breaks through the blocking and threatens the punter. The punt protector then picks a spot to run through–almost like option blocking–but this week we knew exactly where we wanted our protector, Jerry Schwartzberg, to run.

Also, we wanted to kickoff away from their tailback, number 31, who was an excellent kickoff return man.

The game plan was complete; therefore, we spent the following week in practice working on the execution of that game plan. Had we thought of everything? Had we prepared them enough? Had we anticipated correctly what our opponent's game plan would be? We didn't want the accusing finger of our own mental Monday morning quarterbacking to point at mistakes we coaches had made. At that point in time, there was no way to know if we had successfully armed our young warriors for battle.

As the time for the 7 o'clock game on Friday approached, excitement was thick enough to cut with a chainsaw. For the five seniors who had played against Cactus as sophomores in the '96 Playoff game, there was an obvious air of apprehension. They knew from experience how good the Cactus football tradition was: Cactus made the Playoffs every year; they had 50 to 60 kids each year on the varsity; they were big, and always acted extremely confident of winning.

Darren Urban, sports writer for <u>The Tribune Newspaper</u> posted the standings for class 4A and speculated on the Firebirds chances for the season in his "Prep Preview" column:

When Chaparral football coach Ron Estabrook walked off the field for the final time in 1996 – a humbling 35-7 loss to Gilbert to cap a disappointing 5-5 season – he saw a team that had gone backward from its playoff season of 1995.

"We are going back to basics," Estabrook said then. "We are not talking about anything but lifting weights, getting stronger, and learning our jobs."

And so they did.

Armed with a handful of seniors that have been starting since they were sophomores, third-year boss Estabrook now has a team completely made up of players he brought to the varsity. Given the ebb and flow of the other teams in the 4A East Sky Region. This could be the Firebird's year.

"We were thinking of this as a three-year thing, and we're not looking at this as a peak but rather we are hoping we have reached the level of play we want to be at In the future," he said.

It starts on offense, built around third-year starters Scott Johnson at quarterback (1,484 yards passing. 17 TDs) and fullback Jerry Schwartzberg (1,520 yards rushing, 14 TDs).

"What they mean is I have role models and leaders for the younger kids, more than just what they produce on the field," Estabrook said of the two. "They know the system and the attitude they bring to the table is huge for this team."

Joining Schwartzberg in the backfield will be senior Jess Morton and sophomore Josh Griffin, who scored 24 touchdowns on the junior varsity last season. Between Schwartzberg, Griffin and wideout Ryan Cobb, who moves from running back after averaging 24 yards a catch out of the backfield last year, Estabrook feels his team has the speed it needs. John Hogue also will see receiver time, and tight end Adam Goodworth, a senior, was an all-city selection last year. Estabrook's ultimate plan for success means one-way players on both sides of the ball, so he has some decisions to make on linemen like Chris Dobbins (6-0, 250), Clay Muschinski (6-2, 260), Dan Kaufmann (6-2, 250) and Brad Reisner (5-10, 210), who all will see time on both the offensive and defensive lines.

A pair of linebackers, seniors Matt Way and Jake Ireland, also could play some offensive line, though they will anchor the defense, along with fellow linebacker senior David Williams. Mike Reisner and sophomore Austin Sendlein will try and find a spot at linebacker as well.

The defensive backfield is led by junior Zach Bies and senior Larry Zak, with Mike Camello and Matt Willden vying for some playing time.

Estabrook believes last year's troubles are gone. "I don't think we were good enough to win the squeakers last year," he said, adding, "I think that's changed."

His "Outlook" column on Thursday, the day before the game, announced, "And maybe we'll get to see just how good these Firebirds really are. Prediction: Cactus 35, Chaparral 31."

His prediction actually helped us. It waved a banner of challenge–and our kids seemed to thrive on dared challenges.

That night, on the way to the Cactus game, the bus buzzed with excitement. Matt Way wiped sweaty palms on his pants. His stomach felt like he had swallowed a swarm of gnats. He turned in his seat and told Jerry and Jake, "I know we're a better football team than they are, but, you know, they've got that super strong tradition thing. Our tradition's just the opposite. Hangs over our heads..."

They nodded in agreement.

"Maybe we *can* turn around Chaparral's tradition this year. Be awesome if we could."

They didn't seem to want to talk, so he looked out the window as the bus snorted into fifth gear. His nervousness seemed to unbutton his mouth–their's apparently worked in the opposite. *Every person on this team worked hard in the off season,* he told himself. *We paid the price, will it pay off? This game's going to set the pace for the rest of the season.* In response to his own internal pep talk, he said aloud, "Yes!" and formed a fist.

Jerry Schwartzberg confessed to his best friend, Jake Ireland, "I'm really nervous, man!"

"Yeah, well don't think you're alone–me too."

"Problem is...I just don't know how good we are. Glendale wasn't a real good test."

"Yep, but I was wound so tight after that scrimmage I couldn't sleep that night." Jake had a lot to prove–to himself, and the coaches. His enthusiasm had gone south at the end of his junior year. It had started high, and was one of his strongest attributes, but disillusionment with the senior leadership the previous year had affected his game. It turned out to be a chicken and the egg cycle. Poor performance led to additional disappointment in himself. This year, however he was ripe for redemption. Now armed with a new mindset, Jake's determination bristled like quills on a porcupine. He was only one of two players starting on both offense and defense–offensive guard, and middle linebacker. Jake was carrying a double load which would give him plenty of opportunity to prove himself tonight.

As the team exited the bus, dark storm clouds sailed above Cactus high school like swift and menacing pirate ships. Whirls of small "dust devils" created miniature tornadoes of dirt which skipped like Tasmanian devils across the parking lot. I shivered. Was it an omen?

There is a certain comfortable psychology about playing a home game. It has little to do with lines being drawn on a field where constant practice takes place. The comfort zone exists on the playing field of the mind, and is perhaps the same premise which spawned the phrase, "your own turf" as a morale booster. As the Firebirds came onto the field at Cactus, I found myself wishing we could have played this first game on home turf. I would soon find that Cactus would attempt a few additional mind games to rub our nose in the Cactus tradition.

All of a sudden, the Cactus team made their appearance. They marched through the goalposts on the north end of the field. They were approximately sixty strong, resplendent in "Carolina Blue" uniforms with white numerals. We only dressed out about thirty kids. Now, approximately sixty huge, brutal-looking players fell into the formation of a star, and began to chant as they warmed up. It was a deep, guttural mantra of raw intimidation. "Gonna' get 'em...gonna' beat 'em..."

The Firebirds, doing stretches on the south end of the field, pretended not to notice, but they were slightly wide-eyed. Matt Way confessed later that the size of the Cactus team was intimidating. Not only were they big, but they towered over the Firebirds like redwoods. He had never been up against a team that big before.

I leaned toward Ron, "This is like a scene from Spartacus." The gruff, threatening chants reached a higher level as Cactus continued to work out. I was worried it might browbeat the team.

"Cecil B. DeMille would be proud," his tone was dour. "Just hope it doesn't intimidate the team. Hope they ignore it." And then a curious thing happened...As Clay Mushinski stretched, he made the remark, "Yeah, that's really scary."

Jake took up the thread of Clay's sarcasm. In tempo with stretching, in a deep exaggerated voice, he chanted, "Yeah, we're scared...really scared...can't beat us...can't rip us up..." Any hint of intimidation had been broken. Our kids continued to work out as though nothing had happened–but they were all smiling. David's humor had stopped Goliath's taunts.

Ron shot a look in my direction. He smiled and nodded slightly. His eyes said, "Our kids just cooked that raw intimidation."

In the locker room before the game, Ron gave his usual short talk with emphasis on how important the game was, and then Dana fired off a sizzling pep talk that pumped up the excitement and resolve. Even with a bad, sixty year old hip I always had to resist the urge to "suit up" and play, when Dana got everyone's blood racing before a game.

Ryan McConnell, number 31, the Cactus running back and place kicker teed up the ball on the 40 yard line. Jerry Schwartzberg said later he felt his heart was going to explode all over the field as he waited at his up-back position on the 30 yard line.

Josh Griffin, the quick little running back who ran 4.5 in 40 yards, waited together with Ryan Cobb on the 5 yard line for the ball to be kicked. Both were nervous. Butterflies the size of F-16's did "touch and goes" in their stomachs. They reminded each other to "look" the ball into their hands, elbows together, so that the ball wouldn't slip through. We coached "looking the ball" which wasn't exactly imaging it, but more graphically as though the eyes were a magnetic force pulling the ball into their hands.

The referee's whistle shrilly pierced the air.

Ryan McConnell's upraised hand went down, and he approached the ball on the tee as the loud drum roll from the band accentuated his kick. The game was on.

Ryan Cobb, number 23, watched the ball. It somersaulted end over end, coming slowly to his side of the field. Josh Griffin moved in front of him, five yards to his side, and five yards ahead of Ryan. He watched the ball drop into Ryan's hands. If the ball were fumbled, he was ready to pick it up.

Ryan deftly caught the ball and started up field, accelerating, gathering speed with Griffin also running at full tilt. Just as Ryan reached the 35 yard line, he was tackled. A good return. The goal for the special team kickoff return team was to give the ball to the offense on average, at the 35 yard line. Speedsters Cobb and Griffin were ready to keep up that tradition.

The Chaparral Firebirds showed their nervousness on the first snap from scrimmage, where there was a bad exchange from the center–Dan Kaufman to Scott Johnson, the quarterback. The ball dropped on the ground. Scott fell on it for a 2 yard loss.

Scott showed his poise as he patted Kaufman on the back as if to say, "No problem, don't worry about it...everything's okay." Scott was 6' 2", 190 pounds, and had been the starting QB for three years now. He knew the offense inside and out and had been a good leader on and off the field.

Cactus' defensive line was outplaying Chaparral's, and on third down there was an incomplete pass by Scott. It was fourth down. John Hogue got a good punt off–the coverage was excellent after the returner caught the ball and was tackled for a two yard gain.

On Cactus' first offensive play, the quarterback reverse pivoted to his right and handed the ball to his tailback, #31. With the big fullback leading the way, McConnell gained 9 yards over right tackle. Then, a pitch left to McConnell, as he swept his left side for a first down.

Chaparral was still acting nervous. On the next play, a fullback trap up the middle, the Chaparral defensive tackles Brad Reisner and Chris Dobbins closed down the trap for no gain. Dobbins had excellent technique in "cross-hatting" the pulling guard.

"Cross-hatting" is a technique that Coach Zupke teaches which helps the defensive lineman keep the offensive player from getting a blocking angle on him. When the defensive player "cross-hats" the blocker, he squeezes and closes the hole by taking his outside shoulder, and with the same arm ripping through the inside shoulder of the blocker. This closes the gap behind the offensive player and affords the defensive lineman an opportunity to tackle the ball carrier.

On second down, Cactus tried another trap play for the tailback, and Chaparral shut it down again. On third down, the Cactus quarterback faked a draw to McConnell, rolled out to his right, threw to his wide receiver on the sideline. But it was overthrown.

Fourth down–Cactus punted. The wind, which later was clocked at over 30 mph, had not yet started up, and the punt had good distance. It was high enough so that Ryan Cobb, the returner, had to call for a fair catch. But the ball bounced off his fingers. There was a unison moan from the Chaparral stands, but just before the first Cactus player arrived Ryan fell on the ball. Now, a unison sigh of relief emanated from the Chaparral bench and stands behind as though conducted in concert by some choir director.

The Firebirds seriously needed to get a solid drive going—get some offensive rhythm going—put away the butterflies with a confidence producing drive. Coach Estabrook signaled in *32 trap* to Scott. He was signalling for our left guard to pull and block the first defensive lineman to the right side of center. No gain.

"Let's get outside. Inside is too tough," Estabrook said aloud, more to himself than addressing any of us. He hand-signaled *37 blast option,* where the QB fakes a handoff to the left halfback, Griffin, and then quick pitches to the fullback running wide to his left. Even though it's called "37 blast option," it's not really an option. The pitch is pre-determined. Jerry caught the pitch from Scott picking up 9 yards.

Third and one. Jerry takes the ball from Scott, who had pivoted to his left and ran behind the left guard and the left tackle. This was *33 belly* for a first down. Then *34 belly* to the right side—five yards. Next, a fake to Jerry on *33 belly* to the left, and the hand off to Griffin running the *24 counter* back to the right behind the trap block of the big left tackle, Clay Muschinski. Griffin gained 4 yards.

Third and one. Ron thought Cactus would be looking for something up the middle on third and one, so he called *28 waggle,* where the QB opens up to his left, and fakes to the fullback, Schwartzberg, running up the middle right behind the center and then fakes the ball to Griffin, the left halfback, now running to his right. If the QB were to hand the ball to the fullback, it would be either *32 dive* (man-on-man blocking) or *32 trap.* If the quarterback handed the ball to the left halfback on a sweep to the right, it would be *28 sweep.*

The receivers on *28 waggle* run the following patterns: The split end on the left side runs straight down the field, fakes to the inside and then runs a "corner" route—a 45 degree angle to the sideline. The tight end, who is lined up on the right side, comes across the field to the left about 8-10 yards deep on a crossing pattern, and the right running back, lined up as a wingback, runs a "post" pattern down the middle of the field on a deep pattern.

It is a very difficult play action pass to defend. In addition, the fullback, after he fakes into the line, then runs out to his left no deeper than five yards.

On this particular play, Jerry was open and Scott threw the ball right into his hands. He sprinted down the sidelines for 50 yards to the Cactus 20 yard line.

It was the first big play in the game. The Chaparral sidelines exploded.

Next play–*28 sweep*. Griffin almost scored as he gained 17 yards to the three yard line.

First and goal. Scott took one step back from center and fired a quick slant pass to his wide receiver, John Hogue. The ball was thrown too low–incomplete.

Second down. Jerry on *33 belly*. No gain.

Third down. Scott pivoted to his right and handed the ball to Jerry on *34 belly*, off the right tackle–two yard gain.

Fourth and one. Chaparral needed to score badly. A Cactus goal line stand would surely give an encouraging stroke to their nervousness.

Chaparral broke the huddle with a formation which spread the defense. Often offenses will do this on short yardage situations, especially when they want to run up the middle. The Firebirds split out both ends, and then put a halfback on each side about five yards outside the tackles. We called this our "ace" formation (for one set back).

Cactus had to send out two men to each side, leaving seven defensive men to defend what was obviously going to be a run up the middle. Scott took the ball from center, pivoted to his left, and as Jerry came up the middle, faked him the ball. He then handed it to Griffin on *28 sweep* going to his right. Griffin easily ran in for a touchdown behind a good block by Jake Ireland, who pulled and led the way. Adam Goodworth blocked the outside defender.

The Chaparral stands and bench went bonkers. Yells, cheers, whistles and noisemakers exploded like a small mushroom cloud. Cheerleader's crimson and yellow pom poms shook the air defiantly. The band blared the victory song.

Even though Griffin's try for the point was wide left, it didn't damper Chaparral's wild enthusiasm. 6 - 0, Chaparral.

On the following kickoff, we decided to "pooch" the ball up in the air to our left. It hit on the Cactus 30, and as players from both teams scrambled, a Cactus player ended up with the ball on their 25.

Now it was up to the defense to hold them, but Cactus had other ideas. First play, tailback nine yards off tackle. Then 8 yards...then 5 yards up the middle by the fullback. After a few more plays, number 31 ran a counter and broke it to our 10 yard line.

QB rolled out left–5 yard loss.

Then, the tailback on a sweep–3 yards. Third down. The QB slipped on a rollout left.

Fourth down. Big play for both teams, QB rolled right, the wide receiver on that side of the field started down field, across the goal line, turned a couple of steps to the middle of the field, and then ran parallel with the line of scrimmage to the sidelines. There it was–the slash pattern we were so concerned about!

Matt Wilden, our left cornerback, almost got there, but it was a perfect pass–touchdown.

The extra point was good and it was 7-6, Cactus.

The wind was starting to pick up speed now. Lightning to the north proclaimed another Arizona monsoon storm would be bearing down on us.

Cactus had the wind with them. Their kickoff bounced into the end zone, so we started the next drive on our 20 yard line.

On second down, Griffin ran *28 sweep* to the right picking up 28 yards. Then Jerry off right tackle, grabbed 7 yards on *34 belly.* Then, with three wide receivers left, in what we call our "trips" formation, Scott hit Adam Goodworth, our tight end, with a pass for 7 yards on an "out" pattern. The out pattern is when the receiver runs straight down the field for 5-10 yards and cut 90 degrees to the sidelines.

First down. Scott throws again to Goody, trips right, on a "wheel" pattern where he runs on out to the sideline, then wheels up field. The pass was behind Goody. Incomplete.

Second down. Jerry goes up the middle on *31 drive* for 8 yards. Then on *32 trap*, Jerry gained 4 yards for a first down.

Scott then faked *34 belly* to Jerry and pitched the ball to Griffin going around end for 15 yards. After a couple of running plays gained only a couple of yards, Scott again faked the *34 belly* right to Jerry, took a couple of steps and then threw a perfect pass to Ryan Cobb in the end zone. The Cactus defender hit Cobb before he caught the ball, but there was no interference as the ball fell hopelessly to the ground.

Fourth down. Big call. The ball is now on the Cactus 27 yard line with Chaparral lined up in a double tight end formation with both halfbacks lined up in a wing position on their respective sides. It looks like a running formation, but has turned out to be a good passing formation for play action passes.

Griffin starts in motion going from left to right. Scott fakes to Jerry on the trap, and then to Griffin on the *28 sweep*–it's the bootleg pass again–*28 waggle*–Hogue in his tight end position now runs 10 yards, and then cuts to his left on a 45 degree angle. Just as he made his cut, Scott threw him the ball. It was a little long, but Hogue compensates valiantly by diving for the ball. It's complete on the 2 yard line.

Screaming cheers from the stands urge the Firebirds to score. Jerry runs up the middle–touchdown Chaparral. Jerry runs in the extra point for two. Now the scoreboard reads: "Chaparral 14, Cactus 7." My own sweaty palms were beginning to dry out. *So much for raw intimidation!*

Jagged streaks of menacing lightning spiked toward the north. The storm rumbled in the distance like a discontented giant. It was now the second quarter, so when we kicked off we had the advantage of the wind as an invisible player on our team. The ball was kicked into the end zone, and Cactus started on their 20 yard line. They got a first down on their first two plays. Then we held them, forcing them to punt to us.

We took over on our 40 yard line, but after three incomplete passes, we were forced to punt. David Williams, our long snapper for punts had never snapped in a game before. In fact, none of our punters, kickers, holders, or snappers had ever performed their specialty in a varsity game. I held my breath.

David, who did a superb job all year on long snaps for punts and extra points, snapped this one to the right and low to John Hogue. John quickly moved to his right, scooped up the ball like a shortstop, and as he started his steps to punt, saw the blue shirt of a Cactus player coming right up the middle. John kept his cool. He quickly got the ball away, and with the acceleration of the wind, plus a good roll, it went all the way to the Cactus 7 yard line.

It appeared we had Cactus in a hole with just a couple of minutes left in the half. The wind had now developed into a gale of 25 mph, with higher gusts. If the defense could hold, and force Cactus to punt into the wind, Chaparral would have great field position.

Their calculations must have also taken the wind into consideration. On the first play, the Cactus QB took a three step drop and hit his tight end with a perfect pass over the middle. He ran all the way to the 50 yard line before our defensive backs tackled him.

Then, after a penalty against us, #31 broke free on a trap up the middle from 35 yards out for a touchdown. They kicked the extra point, and it was 14-14 with 1:19 minutes left on the clock.

The sudden touchdown, after having Cactus in a hole on their seven yard line, hit the Chaparral bench like a stun gun. The huge home crowd of 4,000 Cactus fans turned on the noise, overpowering the distant thunder.

If Chaparral was going to fold, now would be the time.

Cactus kicked off against the wind. It went on the ground to Cobb, who picked up the ball at the 15, and returned it to our 35. Good field position.

On the first two plays out of our ace formation, Scott got sacked. It was third and 26 on our 19 yard line.

Again, in the ace formation (twin receivers to each side) Scott hit Cobb on a "seam" pattern straight down the field for 29 yards. Chaparral had a first down.

Scott hurried his team to line up after the catch. No huddle–time was running out. We were in our "hurry up" offense.

As Scott was running up the field he looked at Coach Estabrook. Ron signaled in the *draw play*. Scott made sure everyone was set. The ball was snapped–he dropped as if to pass, and handed the ball off to Jerry on the draw. Jerry spotted a hole to his left, right behind Clay Muschinski and Matt Way. He ran straight up field, cut to his right as a Cactus tackler ended up with air in his arms.

Jerry steamed toward the right sidelines, and sprinted a total of 52 yards into the end zone. Ryan Cobb had gotten ahead of Jerry down field, was tempted to block a Cactus player in the back as he turned on him, but held off–it was a heady play–of which he had many over his two year career.

There were just 17 seconds left on the clock. The Chaparral stands reverberated in euphoria. We missed the extra point. The score at halftime was Chaparral 20, Cactus 14. The 52 yard touchdown run by Jerry, with just seconds left, was a massive shot of revitalization for the team and coaching staff.

The Firebirds' confidence took wing as they jogged off the field toward the locker room. The team had definitely overcome the intimidation scene from Spartacus, but now deep rolling thunder to the north began its own ominous chant.

The visitor's locker room was small. As it was just big enough to accommodate 32 players, practically standing in each others armpits, we coaches met outside. While Dana Zupke talked to the defense, Ron waited to meet with the offense.

I took Ron's arm and guided him outside the door where we'd have a measure of quiet.

"I've got an idea," I told him. "I know you like to have the wind at your back in the fourth quarter, but this wind is brutal, Ron. I'm afraid if we give up the wind in the third quarter, we'll lose field position. We won't be able to pass against it. In fact, I don't think we can even get a punt off–it would be like punting into a tornado."

Ron's eyebrows raised quizzically above the tinted glasses. His mouth pursed slightly.

"What do you think about us taking the wind in the third quarter? We're ahead. If we score, we'll be up two touchdowns. Then if we have to punt in the fourth quarter, let's run the fake...right behind left guard. They've had their two guys that line up there bailing out on every one of our punts so far."

He frowned, sifting through, weighing out the strategy. After a few seconds he nodded, "Okay, let's do it–makes sense." He went back into the locker room to talk with the offense.

I got together with Jerry, David Williams, our long snapper, and Josh Utterback, our upback on the left side. I told them what we were going to do in the fourth quarter if we had to punt.

"David, you and Josh...don't just stand there when the ball is snapped to Jerry (rather than the punter). Your guys are going to bail out–go after them. If you do, it's just Jerry and the safety one-on-one."

They seized on the idea, nodding eagerly.

"Jerry, remember the open hole will be to the left of David, okay?"

"Okay." Jerry smiled as though we were conspiring agents of a foreign government. It was a short meeting, but factoring in the wind was definitely a conspiratorial plus.

The stands on both sides went wild as the second half began. It seemed to be a shouting match battle between them. The cacophony of noise and cheers sent pinwheel sparklers of excitement into the air. Bands on both sides of the field began a duel of their own.

We kicked off the second half. Whalers in dripping yellow slickers would have had to lash themselves to the mast in the storm wind which was now behind us. I figured Griffin's kickoff could end up in Tucson–at least be out of the end zone. Wrong. He kicked it to the 2 yard line, but it had a lot of height on it.

When #31, McConnell caught the ball with the wedge forming at the 15, he had no idea what would happen next. Zach Bies, our strong safety, and one of the Firebirds' best special teams players, broke the wedge nailing McConnell on the 12 yard line. It was one of those body-slamming hits you could hear all over the stadium–one you cringingly "felt" vicariously, as well as heard.

Chaparral sidelines and our stands erupted. McConnell looked stunned as he got up. The Cactus star running back had gained 104 yards in the first half. After this astounding tackle, however, which seemed like Bies had stuck a runaway Kamatsu bulldozer up his sleeve during halftime, McConnell ended up only gaining 19 yards in the second half.

Cactus now got a first down on a play action pass, then Jake Ireland sacked the QB on a blitz by the middle linebacker.

After a draw for no gain on second down, and a rollout by the QB for five yards, Cactus punted on fourth down. It was a 20 yard punt against the wind, but we were called for roughing the punter—a ticky-tack penalty, he was hardly touched.

First down, Cactus, on the 50 yard line. Had the momentum changed? On the first play the Cactus QB rolled right—the receivers were covered, and he started running...45...40...down to the 35 yard line. And then Matt Willden, the cornerback on that side, stripped him of the ball. The ball rolled loose, toward the sideline, and Michael Camello, the free safety, fell on the ball. A huge break for Chaparral.

The Firebird award winning Varsity Cheer Line and Varsity Poms danced and whirled leading the fans in a roaring, triumphant cheer. Both squads pumped the enthusiasm.

Chaparral then moved the ball down the field in seven aggressive running plays to the Cactus 12. The biggest gain was on *31 trap* up the middle with Jerry gaining 20 yards to start the drive. But on fourth and one, Cactus held.

First down–Cactus. But we held them, and now forced to punt against the wind, with the Firebirds pressuring the kicker, the punt fizzled for just 15 yards.

The Chaparral offensive machine went to work on the Cactus 44 yard line–Jerry over right tackle on *34 belly* for nine yards.

Then, out of the "trips" formation, it was Jerry grabbing six yards, running hard like a spirited thoroughbred. On the next play he almost broke it, picking up 15 yards on *37 pitch*, running left away from the trips–the offensive formation of 3 receivers lined up to one side.

Next play, *28 waggle*, which resulted in an incomplete pass to Hogue.

Third down, *33 belly*–a loss of four.

Fourth down from the 20. This down was key. If Cactus held here a second time, it could turn the momentum of this 20-14 game. I knew God didn't "choose up sides" in a ball game, but I said a swift prayer anyway.

Wing left–Scott takes the ball from center, fakes to Jerry up the middle, and then to Ryan Cobb on the sweep left, *47 waggle*. As he bootlegged to his right, Scott saw Hogue was covered in the right corner. He then looked for his secondary receiver, the tight end, coming left-to-right across the middle. Goody read the defensive secondary correctly and broke deep into the end zone. Scott hit him perfectly for the TD.

I secretly hoped the Cactus visitor's stands were ruggedly reinforced–our Chaparral fans were testing their strength by jumping up and down. The din was deafening.

The two point conversion failed when Scott didn't pitch on the option and was tackled just short of the goal line–Chaparral 26, Cactus 14.

Just a twelve point lead over Cactus and their explosive offense, with an entire quarter to go, was precarious. In 22 seconds the Cactus Cobras would have the wind, which would give them the dangerous venom to strike. No one was relaxing in the Chaparral camp.

With 22 seconds left in the quarter, Griffin kicked off into the end zone. Cactus had to start their drive on their 20. On the first play Cactus ran a fullback trap for 14 yards.

First down and the quarter was over. Now, they had the wind.

First down again and a handoff to their tailback, out of the "I" formation, running to his right for 6 yards.

Second down resulted in a quick pass down the middle which Camello deflected–incomplete.

Big third down play–another key play: the QB pivots to his left, pitching the ball to #31, McConnell. Jake Ireland, on a blitz from his middle linebacker spot, hammered him for a 5 yard loss.

Fourth down, and the crisis wasn't over–they were punting with the wind which could easily gain great field position pinning us inside our 20.

The Firebirds punt block team put on a great rush, forcing the Cactus punter to kick the ball straight up in the air. When it finally stopped rolling, it had gone a grand total of 15 yards. Chaparral now had the great field position.

One more score would put this game out of reach. Griffin gained 20 yards on third down on a counter. However, a holding penalty and two other plays, of a loss and no gain, sandwiched between a five yard *33 belly* by Jerry, now found Chaparral with fourth down and 12 on our own 41 yard line. We would be punting against the wind.

The punted ball would probably carry only 10-15 yards tops, leaving Cactus in great field position, plenty of time to perform with 6:57 minutes remaining, and only trailing 26-14. The factors which Ron and I had discussed at halftime were now in place.

As the punt team left the sidelines, my eyes silently quizzed Ron.

"Go for it," he said, never hesitating.

"Davy," I grabbed David Williams by the arm. "Fake punt, punt protector run." As he started to run onto the field I yelled, "Remind Jerry and Utterback."

He nodded and ran toward the huddle. Would it work?

As the punt team broke the huddle on our 41 and lined up, drum rolls began in my stomach. My dry throat was testimony to the fact that when assistant coaches make recommendations which are risk-oriented, they're under "G" force pressure.

We don't get the credit if it works, the head coach does–and that's the way it should be. If it doesn't work, however, the head coach isn't going to pass that buck and tell the press he wasn't responsible for a disastrous play decision. The head coach takes the heat, but there is usually a trickle-down effect of reminders at some later date.

I held my breath as Jerry, the punt protector, lined up behind the right guard, five yards behind the line of scrimmage. As David snapped the ball to Jerry, John Hogue, who was lined up 13 yards behind the line of scrimmage, jumped up in the air, pretending that it was a bad snap over his head.

Jerry caught the center snap, paused for a second to let his blockers form, and then headed to the left of center behind Josh Utterback. Jake Ireland, the player next to Utterback, drove into his man and turned him out.

Yes! Just as we had predicted, Utterback's and Williams' men started backing off the line. As Jerry tore through the huge hole on his left, Utterback and Williams caught up with the two men and blocked them. Jerry now cut to his right, about ten yards beyond the line of scrimmage. There was just one man between him and the goal line–the Cactus returner, who started moving up towards Jerry. Jerry gave him a little fake to the left and accelerated up field. No contest–he scored easily. Our kids executed it beautifully.

The jubilation on the sidelines was almost matched by the Chaparral players themselves as they mobbed Jerry in the end zone.

It was the back breaker–the morale cruncher for Cactus–the turning point in the game. Griffin ran it over for the two point conversion on *28 sweep*. It was now 34-14. Ron gave me a smiling thumbs up.

On the ensuing kickoff the wind was so powerful, one of the Chaparral players had to hold the ball for Griffin. He kicked it to the Cactus 25 where they fell on it. Larry Zak, our left corner, made a great play on third down...they had to punt.

So far, no scores for Cactus in the second half. Dana Zupke had made two important adjustments at halftime:

Our ends were getting blocked on their counter, and he reminded them very forcefully to come underneath those blocks. He stressed that our ends had to use the technique of "cross-hatting."

The second adjustment was to move the two outside linebackers from five yards deep, up to one yard from the line of scrimmage. This still left the middle linebacker five yards deep and free to flow with the play. They hadn't been hurting us outside with their speed–it was the pounding of their two big backs, running between the tackles, which was hurting us.

It was now fourth down. We decided to keep our defense on the field, not put a returner back deep. Two things: if they ran a fake we were going to need all eleven of our players, and if they did punt, we didn't want to take a chance on our returner mishandling that punt. We were playing it safe all the way.

There was no fake, and with no pressure the punter got off a good punt. The wind caught it, and for a moment it looked like it might take off for Oz, but it finally rolled dead at our ten yard line. After three running plays, we had not gained the necessary yardage. The ball was on our 14. We didn't want to punt into the wind, so we sent word in to Scott to take the snap from center and run out of the end zone. At first no one, including our players and the fans, understood what was going on.

When we lined up for the kickoff from our 20 yard line, it was quickly understood. We had purposely taken a safety so that we would have a free kick from our 20 yard line. This was a prudent option rather than punt against a vicious wind, which seemed to have decided it wanted to take over the game. It was now Chaparral 34, Cactus 16.

We huddled up before the kickoff and I told Griffin to pooch left. I also told David Williams, "Davy, you can get the ball–that wind is going to make it tough for them to get it and they won't be expecting it." I punched him lightly on the shoulder. "You can do it."

Again, the wind was so powerful Matt Willden had to hold the ball in order for Griffin to kick it.

He pooched the ball to his left about 20 yards downfield, but as the Cactus player came forward to catch the ball, the wind blew it back towards David Williams. The ball hit the ground just past the outstretched fingertips of the frustrated Cactus player and....Davy fell on it. "Great!" I yelled.

Three plays later, Griffin scored on *28 sweep* by sprinting 59 yards for a final touchdown. David Williams tacked on 2 more points as he ran *45 power* off of left tackle.

Fans shot onto the field like a fountain of fireworks spewing a flood of crackling excitement. Through the screaming hilarity, coaches shook hands–players shook hands. I thought I might have to shop for a hearing aid...soon.

Everybody tried to talk at the same time on the bus trip back to Chaparral. The team was really "up." They deserved to be–they'd played a great game.

The following morning The Tribune headline read, "Birds: Chaparral Rushes for 348 Yards vs. Cobras." The Arizona Republic column read: "Ill Wind for Cactus/Chaparral's Runners Rack up 5 TD's in Rout."

Our offense had rolled to 479 total yards while holding Cactus to 156 yards. Jerry Schwartzberg had rushed for 212 yards in 28 carries for a 7.6 yard average. Josh Griffin had rushed for 147 yards in 12 carries for a 12.3 yard average. What a terrific game for the little sophomore, who was only 5'8" and 170 pounds. He had scored three TD's in this, his first varsity game.

Of course the team reveled in the praise of the newspaper headlines; however the next morning Coach Estabrook wrote his own headline on the blackboard in the team room: "The Good, The Bad, and The Ugly." After looking at the game film earlier that morning he was right. We had some "good" plays, but we also had seen some "bad," and as usual in a first game, some "ugly." We had a lot of work to do.

Our hope was that the kids wouldn't let this victory go to their heads. The score was not indicative of how close the game really was. Until the fake punt, with just under seven minutes, and Cactus being behind by only 12 points with a 30 mile gale at their backs–it was still anybody's game. We had gotten some good breaks, particularly a big "blow hard" who had decided he wanted to be a team player...the wind.

With that in mind, the coaching staff now tackled the problem of how to communicate to our kids just how tough the next game against Centennial would be. Our instruction should be a balancing act of walking the tightrope between encouragement and discipline. We needed to push the right buttons to praise them highly for what they had just accomplished, without letting the team become over-confident.

To put a damper on any over-confidence, Ron planned to refer to this game in his later summation to the team as "The Good, the Bad and the Ugly." He hoped to squelch presumptions which could lead to improper preparation for the Centennial game. Ron's psychology was like that of a general finely attuned to his troops–over-confidence can lead to ambush. He wanted his warriors armed and ready, and as it turned out Centennial was tougher than Cactus–a lot tougher.

THE TURNAROUND

CHAPTER FOUR

"33 BELLY AND 'D'"

The Saturday morning after the Cactus game, Coach Estabrook scrawled in heavily chalked letters on the blackboard, "The Good, The Bad, and the Ugly." He crossed his arms and viewed the team. There was silence in the room, and several lifted eyebrows. "Put your seat belts on. I want you to come back down to earth after your fantastic win."

There were several grins...some squirming.

"We know about the good. I'm issuing a challenge for us to take a good hard look at the bad and the ugly. We need to get the passing game going. The Cactus game was certainly not a litmus test of what we were capable of doing passing-wise."

Scott Johnson, who had thrown well in passing league games and in his sophomore and junior years, had only completed 5 for 13 and 103 yards with one touchdown. Granted, the wind had been a definite factor. Several times he had not thrown the ball and taken sacks, but the coaches were hopeful that the Centennial game would be his "breakout" game. We knew that we had a great running game with our fast backs and our offensive line, which seemed to be improving in practice each week; however, we needed to have a balanced offense, and to do that, we needed the passing game to be successful. Ron told us that Scott's father,

Chuck Johnson, had called Darren Urban to complain about the publicity that Scott was getting. Darren had apparently written something to the effect that Chaparral's passing game was disappointing.

Jerry Schwartzberg claimed, "The Cactus game is going to set the pace of the rest of the season."

Matt Way was perhaps more conservative. He felt that, "Centennial is as good as Cactus and I'm worried that we're overlooking them. If we underestimate them, we're going to get beat." He frowned at his own assessment. He had watched the film of the Centennial - Coronado game, and it was obvious they had a very solid defense.

Coronado had won in a game which had the same wind effects that Chaparral had with Cactus. Coronado had upset Centennial, however, the week before by a 12-0 score, but Centennial had been inside Coronado's 5 yard line three times and couldn't score.

One time, a Coronado defensive back intercepted the Centennial QB at the goal line and returned it 76 yards. On the next play, the great Coronado running back, Joel Huerta, ran 24 yards for the score. Huerta also broke another long run to set up the second TD. Other than those two plays, Centennial had totally dominated Coronado. With turnovers and eight penalties for 60 yards, Centennial had shot itself in the proverbial foot.

Continuing to poll the players for their comments, we found that Clay Muschinski felt the coming game was important to him. He revealed he did not feel he had played well in the Cactus game. He wasn't happy with the grade which the offensive line coach, Dana Zupke, had given him—but he knew that it was a fail game grade. This game against Centennial was going to be his coming out week.

Adam Goodworth admitted he had been concerned about Cactus. He remembered how strong their defensive linemen had been two years ago in the playoff game. At halftime during the Cactus game, however, he had felt confident Chaparral would win. He could move their defensive linemen when he blocked them.

He now expressed confidence that we would win against Centennial.

Jake Ireland told us the Cactus game had been a "redemption" game. He felt he had a lot to prove. The entire off-season, from December to August, he had been focused on getting ready to play this football season—not just physically, but mentally. He had gotten off to a great start with a sack and a tackle behind the line of scrimmage for a loss of 5 yards. He led the team in tackle points with 14 (2 points for an unassisted tackle, and 1 point for an assisted tackle).

Zach Bies was right behind him with 12, and David Williams had 11. Jake was confident that we were going to beat Centennial—"beat them real big!"

Coach Zupke was especially concerned with Centennial's huge offensive and defensive line which averaged well over 250 pounds per man. Chaparral's offensive line averaged just under 220 pounds, with just two 250 pounders, a tackle, Muschinski and the center, Dan Kaufman.

There were also two 190 pounders— guards, Jake Ireland and Matt Way. A junior, Mike Reisner, 190 pounds, alternated with Matt Way at offensive guard, and started at linebacker. By the middle of the year, Way only played defense and Mike Reisner, our "Iron Man," played both ways. He was our only player to start and play on both the offense and defensive teams. Ellie Davis, the right tackle, and Adam Goodworth, the tight end, only weighed 210 pounds.

Coach Zupke was not only concerned about the huge discrepancy in the size of the two lines, but he was also anxious about the match up of Centennial's nose guard, who was 6'5" and weighed 280 pounds, and according newspaper accounts, ran the 40 in 4.6. (He was later recruited by Nebraska and signed a letter of intent to play there). He would be playing opposite our center, Dan Kaufman, who had shown promise these first few weeks, but Coach Zupke wasn't sure whether Kaufman could handle a defensive player of that caliber. And if Dan couldn't handle him, our offense was going to be "in a world of hurt."

As the defensive coordinator, Dana Zupke was not too concerned about Centennial's offense. It is difficult to discern in just watching game film of an opponent, just how fast their running backs really are. He wasn't too worried about Centennial's team speed, or their running back's speed. Little did he know at the time, he was in for a big surprise.

Head coach, Ron Estabrook, who was also the offensive coordinator, drilled the offense relentlessly all week on getting the passing game going. Kaufman also required special attention from Coach Heideman all week, and in our offensive team period, Brad Reisner, who was only 5'10", 205 pounds, played the role of the Centennial nose guard— Reisner's fleet quickness gave Kaufman a fit.

By Wednesday, you could see Kaufman gaining more and more confidence. The competitive fire of our outstanding sophomore defensive tackle, Reisner, was forcing Kaufman to rise above whatever level he had previously been playing. (Brad Reisner made first team All Conference defensive tackle, and Don Kaufman made the All Conference first team as the offensive center).

Coach Estabrook made one change in his offensive personnel to help the passing game, and it was a significant one. He moved Ryan Cobb with his 4.52 speed in the 40 from right halfback to wide receiver, and was planning on alternating Chris Medill and David Williams in Cobb's place. David was also playing a lot at linebacker. John Hogue, who had started the Cactus game at wide receiver, had great hands, but not great speed. He was more of a "possession" receiver. Coach Dennis Riccio and I coached the receivers, Dennis focusing on the wide receivers, and I more on the tight ends and the overall passing game, including the running backs.

Ron asked us what we thought about Cobb. It was late Saturday afternoon after the Cactus game. We had finished our game plan for Centennial and now we were discussing personnel and personnel changes.

I responded. "Cobb gives us more speed–he's got great hands, he will stretch the defense more than Hogue, but I think Dennis and I are partial to Hogue if we are going to run the ball. He can block. He's the best "stalk" blocker downfield of any receiver that I've seen here at Chaparral in the past seven years. What do you think, Dennis?"

Dennis responded. He didn't speak out very often on his own, but if asked, he always had an opinion, and usually a good one. "If we're going to pass more, to keep a good balance in our offense, say 15 to 20 times a game, then I think that Cobb should be out there."

"Well, we need to throw the ball well," Ron said. "I'm concerned that if we don't throw enough teams will gang up on Griffin and Schwartzberg. How do you think Cobb will handle it—being moved again?" he asked us.

"You know," I responded. "I don't think Ryan cares whether it's running back or wide receiver as long as he feels like he contributes. He's too good an athlete to sit around, he wants the ball and he's got a lot of pride. He doesn't feel he's contributing to the team at wide receiver." Ryan had averaged over six yards a carry the year before as a junior, and over 25 yards per catch as a receiver out of the backfield.

"Okay, it's decided," Ron said. "Cobb goes to wide receiver. We need to get Medill and Williams ready." David Williams, at 5'11", 190 pounds was Schwartzberg's backup at fullback, but he was a heady, smart player who would learn the right halfback position very quickly. Medill, a junior, was 6'0", 180 pounds, ran the 40 in 4.6, and like Williams had good physical courage, and they were both good blockers.

Darren Urban, in the <u>Tribune</u> before the Centennial game commented:

> "Okay, it looks like the Firebirds are for real. Very real. Not only did they beat Glendale Cactus last week, but they dominated in a 42-16 win, and that was without a passing game, done in because of the strong, swirling winds. As long as the weather holds out tonight, and quarterback Scott Johnson can throw unimpeded, the Firebirds offense will be that much more explosive—

hard to believe after Jerry Schwartzberg and Josh Griffin combined for 359 yards against the Cobras.

Centennial will be looking to salvage its start after Coronado shocked them last week. An 0-2 beginning isn't death, but in a region with Agua Fria, Cactus and Peoria, it's going to be tough to win the division. The Coyotes will have to cut down on numerous mistakes.

It would seem that the only thing that could stop Chaparral right now would be over-confidence. Schwartzberg swore after last week that it won't happen, but that doesn't mean it won't.

Prediction: Chaparral 30, Centennial 21."

The week went by quickly. It was 7 o'clock Friday night. The stands were filled on the Chaparral side and Centennial had brought enough of their fans to fill up the visitors side.

Centennial kicked off and then held us on four downs forcing Hogue to punt. Williams, after snapping the ball, got down the field first and forced the returner to start running to his left. Seemingly, out of nowhere, Jarrad Pavkov made a crushing tackle on the Centennial returner at their own 10 yard line.

Chaparral held and forced Centennial to punt. Cobb returned it 8 yards to the Centennial 48. After a couple of plays, Scott hit Griffin on a pass for a first down. After a holding call, Scott dropped back in the pocket, felt pressure and ran for no gain. After another incomplete pass it was fourth down and 12 from the Centennial 42.

Griffin, who was doing the kickoffs and extra points, was also an excellent punter. But because of all the other things that he had going on as a runner, pass receiver, and kicker, we had decided to let him be the backup to Hogue on punting. And if we were inside the other team's 40 yard line and wanted to punt we would put Griffin in for Hogue to punt. That gave us the flexibility to run Griffin on a fake punt around either end.

And that's what we decided to do here. Griffin, with a great second effort, gained 15 yards on the fake punt, running around right end.

First down on the 27. On first down, Scott dropped back in the pocket to throw, started shuffling his feet to the left, and then ran—no gain.

Second down, incomplete pass.

Third down, *43 counter* to David Williams for seven yards.

Fourth and 2. Hand off to Jerry. Gain of one. Centennial took the ball over on downs.

Chaparral had no rhythm in its offense, and frustration was setting in. We needed to get the passing game going.

Second quarter. After forcing Centennial to punt, Chaparral started its next drive on its own 44 after a five yard return by Cobb.

First down. Coach Estabrook was still trying to get the passing game going. "Let's try a play action pass on first down," he said to Scott on the sidelines. *"47 waggle."* On *47 waggle* Scott opens to his right, fakes the ball to the fullback up the middle, then fakes it to the right halfback on a sweep left and then rolls out to his right. Just the opposite of *28 waggle.* After the fullback fakes through the line, he breaks out into the right flat running parallel to the line of scrimmage.

Jerry was open and Scott hit him. Jerry just kept running down the sidelines until he was forced out of bounds after a 17 yard gain.

Ron went to a double tight end (no wide receiver) with both halfbacks lined up one yard outside the ends as wingbacks. Against their five man line it gave us an extra blocker and balanced out our offense a little bit more.

First and 10 from the Centennial 39. *32 trap* and the offensive line behind Matt Way's trap block sprang Jerry for 16 yards. Jerry was running hard, knocking down defensive backs with his irrepressible way of running.

Double tight formation. *28 waggle*, and Scott completes it to Goody for 5 yards.

Second and five. *35 trap* again, as Way again makes the trap block, and Kaufman handles the big noseguard lined up opposite him. Jerry picks up 11 yards, as he almost pops it for a TD. After a penalty, Scott threw to Medill in the end zone—incomplete.

Second down from the 14. Scott takes the ball from center and reverse pivots to his left, faking the ball to Jerry on *33 belly*–the defense, obviously keying off of Jerry, flows to the 3 hole, off of our left tackle. Scott then hands the ball to Griffin who follows the left tackle, Clay Muschinski, who has pulled to his right. Griffin cuts behind the devastating trap block, breaks right to the outside and runs the necessary 14 yards for a TD, standing up.

The extra point is good by Griffin. Chaparral had finally found its offensive rhythm. 7-0.

Centennial got a drive of its own going and moved all the way to the Chaparral 27 yard line before stalling. As they lined up for a 44 yard field goal, I felt sure that we could block it. Even though we get to scout our opponents on film for special teams, I still take the time before each game during warm-ups to scout the other team's specialists when they come out early onto the field to warm up. (See Appendix for "Special Teams Game Chart.")

It's really a very simple operation. I take my stop watch and time how long it takes the other team's center to snap the ball to the punter. I then time how long it takes the punter to get rid of the ball. If it takes longer than 2.5 seconds, I feel that we have a chance to block it. (We work with our long snapper and punter to make sure that we can get the ball off in 2.1 seconds. We have not had a punt blocked in the past 3 years.)

I also clock the hang time of the opponent's punter. If it consistently is short and high, with a hang time of 4.0 or better, then we will have a hard time returning the punt. If the punt, conversely, is low and long, with a hang time of 3.5, then I know we have a good chance to return it. I time the kickoff hang times and what yard line the kicker consistently kicks the ball to, so that I can tell my returners where to line up. I then time the opponents extra point and field goal kicker on how long it takes him to kick the ball. (We like to get it off in 1.35 seconds, but no longer than 1.5 seconds).

I had noticed during their warm-ups that their kicker was consistently taking longer than 1.5 seconds. I knew that with a good rush we could block a field goal if they attempted one, even though their kicker had good range and was making them consistently from the 45 yard line. During our stretching and warm-up period, before the game, I usually go to the returners, Griffin and Cobb, and tell them where to line up. I then go to David williams and Jake Ireland, who are the designated field goal and punt blockers. Anyone can block a kick for us, but we have designed special situations for them to be our blockers.

In the Cactus game, Jake had not really gotten off the ball quickly on their extra points and made the needed effort to block their kicks. The following Saturday, during the team film meeting, I had said to Jake," You wanted me to put you on all of the special teams this year, and I did, but you're not performing the way that you can. You've got one more game." I knew that Jake would respond to a challenge. And he did.

The ball was placed down by the Centennial holder on the right hash mark, seven yards behind the line of scrimmage on the 34 yard line, and with the added 10 yards of end zone it would be a 44 yard attempt. As the ball was snapped, Jake got a great jump, broke between the end and the wingback, reached up and blocked the field goal. The ball went straight down, and we recovered it there on our 36 yard line. None of us knew at the time, but it was a very important play in the game.

As Jake ran off the field, Jake hollered at me, "Coach Mottley, that one's for you!" I laughed and gave him a "high five."

First down. Scott hit Medill on an out in the right flat for 8 yards.

Second and two. Ace formation. Both ends split out wide and both halfbacks in the slot on their side between the ends and the tackles. Scott dropped back, ran out of the pocket and threw the ball poorly to Cobb, about 7 yards off the mark.

Third down. Ron called our "trips" formation–three receivers to the right. Scott faked to Jerry up the middle, then Griffin running to the right, and then Scott rolled out left–*28 waggle,* but Centennial had blitzed on the passing down and the linebacker sacked Scott. It wasn't Scott's fault, just not enough blockers.

Hogue punted on fourth down to the Centennial 23. On first down their QB dropped back and threw into the right flat...right into our free safety, Michael Camello's hands. But he didn't look the ball into his hands–he looked up...and dropped it.

The sidelines groaned along with our fans. It was a sure TD– and we needed it. This game was too close, 7-0, late in the second quarter. We needed to put Centennial away quickly and we weren't getting it done.

A sack by Pavkov and Centennial was forced to punt. Fair catch by Cobb on our 48 yard line.

First down. *38 pitch* to Jerry on a sweep around our right end. It looked like he scored, but the official on our sideline said that he stepped out of bounds on the 22. Then the back judge started waving his arm to bring the ball back. One of our linemen was caught holding down field.

First down again, this time on our 44. Jerry runs for 13 yards on *33 belly* behind Muschinski and Way.

Second down. Scott drops back to pass. For some reason, he short-armed it, and it drops harmlessly to the ground. Scott didn't seem to be throwing with confidence.

Third down. Ron calls a draw to Jerry up the middle and he runs for 25 yards all the way to the 15.

First down. David Williams, in his right halfback spot, goes in motion to the left, at the snap of the ball runs downfield five yards and then breaks toward the sidelines. Scott throws low to him. Incomplete.

Second down. Ace formation. Scott is rushed hard and sacked by their right end.

Third down. The clock is running down. Less than a minute. Scott drops back and throws down the left sideline to Cobb on a fade pattern, but the ball is short, and the Centennial cornerback catches it, but then it slips through his hands. Incomplete.

Fourth down. Ron calls the "old reliable" pass play–*28 waggle*, but everybody is covered and Scott is sacked.

The half is over. Chaparral 7, Centennial 0.

Our locker room at halftime did not look like a winner's locker room. The whole team, along with the coaches were totally frustrated. The passing game we were trying to establish was totally "out of sync."

The coaches were all in agreement that we should run the ball the second half and try to get our passing game straightened out sometime in the future. Ron had called 16 passes, of which there were four sacks, four completions and eight incompletions, for a total of only 35 yards. We had lost 21 yards on sacks, so we had only 14 net yards on 16 pass plays, less than one yard a play. For the game, Chaparral had 353 yards rushing on 42 attempts for an average of 8.4 yards per rush.

You didn't have to be a rocket scientist to make the decision Ron Estabrook made, "We are only going to run the ball this half," he told the offensive linemen at halftime. For Clay Muschinski that was music to his ears. He was ready. He knew that he could handle his man on *33 belly*. "Coach, run *33 belly* behind Matt and me. I guarantee it–we'll eat 'em up."

Ron nodded his head. The strategy, a very simple one, was set.

But before they could execute their simple strategy, Centennial came out with their own simple strategy. After four running plays, they scored a TD on a 21 yard sweep to the left. The extra point was good. 7-7.

Griffin dropped the Centennial kickoff, picked it up and returned it to the 8. But four plays later on our 38, Jerry fumbled. It was a shock to the Chaparral sidelines. We were all stunned. Jerry very seldom fumbled.

The Centennial players were jumping up and down and yelling. The momentum had definitely swung their way. We were in a dogfight.

On the first play from scrimmage Mike Strock, their QB, took a three step drop and lofted the ball to his right. The wide receiver on that side had simply run straight downfield on a fade pattern and gotten behind our left cornerback Matt Willden by two steps. The ball was perfectly thrown. A 38 yard TD pass.

The extra point was good. We were down 14-7. They had scored two TD's within three minutes of the start of the half.

As I got the kickoff receive team together on the sideline, I was looking at all the kids' eyes. I was looking for fear, or discouragement. But I didn't see it. I looked hard at Jerry, who was on that team. He had that "steely" look that he could get in his eyes when things were tough.

I felt better. "All right. Let's get it together. We're better than they are. Let's pop one–good return–everybody gets their man. Let's turn this momentum around. Give the ball to the offense in scoring position." It was my usual little speech, but I felt that I had their attention this time.

The kickoff came to Griffin on the 2. He started up the middle, and at about the 40 yard line, angled for the right sideline. The Centennial safety finally tackled him on their 30 yard line. Griffin had returned it 68 yards. We were in business.

But, hold it! Penalty. Back came the ball to our 17 yard line. The momentum had changed though. The little running back seemed to kick in the energy charge that we needed.

First down. *33 belly* behind big Clay and Matt Way for 45 yards to the Centennial 42.

First down. *33 belly* again for 8 yards to the Centennial 34 yard line.

Second down. *33 belly* for 2 yards to the 32–just short of the first down.

Third down. *33 belly* for 4 yards to the 19 yard line.

First down. *Fake 33 belly, 24 counter* to the right side. Griffin behind Clay's trap block for 5 yards.

Second down. Zach Bies, our strong safety and backup running back, at 6'2", 190 pounds replaced Griffin. Coach Estabrook wanted a big back to lead block the linebacker on *33 belly*. Zach blocked the linebacker as Jerry gains 5 yards to the 7 yard line.

First down. Again, attacking the left side behind Goodworth and Clay, and Jerry's block on the defensive end, Medill runs *35 power* in for a TD.

Griffin missed the extra point. 14-13, favor of Centennial, but Chaparral was now on a roll–just "plain ole smashmouth football." And our kids were loving it.

Griffin kicked off to the 5 yard line, our coverage was good, and we pinned the receiver on their 14 yard line. Five plays later, they punted, and we started our offense machine rolling again, this time from our 39.

First down. Again, *33 belly*. Jerry ran for 35 yards to the Centennial 28, where they finally forced him out of bounds. Bies was in there now, taking on their big, 6'3", 248 pound linebacker. Bies was fearless as he moved him out on every play.

First down. *33 belly* again for 16 yards to the 12 yard line.

First down. Griffin in for Bies. Scott fakes the ball to Jerry on *33 belly* and hands the ball to Griffin on *24 counter*. Clay pulls and traps the opposite tackle. It's a beautiful block and Griffin blows straight up the middle like a runaway train, untouched, for a touchdown. 19-14.

Extra point. We need two. Scott quick pitches to Griffin to the left on *27 pitch* and Griffin covers the three yards easily. 21-14.

Griffin kicks off to the 5 again, and Pavkov breaks through to make a slashing tackle on the 13. We've got great field position.

It's the fourth quarter now. And the real excitement is about to begin.

We stopped them on their first series of the quarter, forcing them to punt. On fourth down, the snap was a little high and to the right. The punter sees the rush coming and decides quickly to run away from the hard rush on his right; he runs to his left. Josh Utterback, who is the right end on the punt block team, what we call our "number 10 man," hit his man, the outside lineman, trying to hold him up on his coverage of the punt; he then turned to run down field. He is the first man down and sets up for the punt returner.

There was only one problem. Josh left too soon. He is not supposed to leave until the ball is punted. So when the punter started running to his left, no one was there. It looked like he was going to make a first down–right there in front of our bench–but Jake literally seemed to come out of nowhere to tackle the punter on the sideline, just a yard shy of the first down. Another big play by Jake.

First down. By now, there should have been no doubt what play the Chaparral Firebirds would run. Yes, *33 belly*! Jerry was getting sick of *33 belly* and tiring rapidly. He told us later he said to himself, "I need to score so I can get some rest." Jerry ran 34 yards for a TD, cutting back to his right and scoring easily. Most players would have taken themselves out of the game. Griffin kicked the extra point. The momentum was Chaparral's at the sidelines, the band playing the fight song, and the fans exploded. 28-14. But this game was not over. Not by a long shot. Another good, high kickoff by Griffin to the 5 and the returner just barely got to the 15.

On second down, the QB had a slot formation to his left. He sent the slot back in motion to his right. We were in man-to-man coverage and that took our safety out of that area as he went with the motion man. It left their receiver one-on-one with our right cornerback Larry Zak. The QB faked the ball to his tailback running off right tackle, then reversed his direction, and began rolling to his left. His wide receiver started to the middle of the field on a post pattern, and then cut to the left corner at a 45 degree angle. The pattern, run out of the I formation, was very similar to our *28 waggle*. The QB then lofted a perfect pass to his receiver. Larry had him covered, the receiver was just a step behind him, but Larry, only 5'8", jumped too soon instead of running through the receiver to try and strip him of the ball. The receiver caught the ball and was gone. Camello finally caught him at the 1 yard line.

On the next play, the QB just took the ball from the center and ran right behind him for the TD. 28-20.

Next was the extra point. Normally, you would kick the extra point making the score 28-21, and then if you scored again making it 28-27, as a coach you would have a decision to make: kick it to tie the game, or take a chance and go for two–win or lose.

But the Centennial coaching staff made an interesting decision. They decided to go for the two points right now, and not wait until the next touchdown. The QB took the snap from center, stepped back one step, and threw a quick pass to his right tight end over the middle. Complete. And we were in what is known as a "barn burner." 28-22, with Chaparral just barely hanging on.

Centennial kicked off out of bounds on our 30, which automatically gave us the ball on our 35.

First down. Yes, *33 belly* again. Jerry gained 13 yards to our 48 yard line.

First down. *24 counter.* Griffin gained only 3 yards, although Clay had another great trap block.

Second down. Centennial knew that we weren't going to throw now, and brought their safety up to the line of scrimmage at our 3 hole. We ran *33 belly* again, but there were too many defenders there. Jerry gained only 1 yard.

Third down. Jerry up the middle on *32 trap*. But he ran to his left instead of cutting to his right behind a great trap block by Matt Way. He only gained 1 yard.

Fourth down. All John Hogue had to do was to punt his usual high 35 yard punt with his 3.6 hang time, and with our good punt coverage Centennial would be pinned inside their 20 with just a couple of minutes to go. We should have great field position.

But Hogue looked up just as he was punting the ball–he shanked the ball off the side of his foot over to our bench–out of bounds–13 yards. A large collective groan went up in the Chaparral stands.

Centennial took over on their own 38. They now had the momentum. They had just scored and now had great position on their own 38 after the shanked punt. And if they could score again, all they had to do was kick the extra point for a 29-28 win.

A confident Centennial team broke the huddle and lined up. First down. Incomplete pass.

Second down. QB rolled to his left and threw to his receiver on a crossing route–15 yards to the Chaparral 37 yard line.

First down. Sweep right. The tailback almost broke it, but Willden and Camello tackled him on our 14.

First down. Sweep left this time, but the tailback fumbles it and tries to pick it up. We have a chance to recover it, but the runner finally falls on the ball. Loss of 6 to the 20 yard line.

Second down. Crossing pass pattern, but Camello breaks it up.

Third down. A pass down the middle at the goal line. Willden does a great job breaking it up. But, no, it's pass interference. The ball is now on the 10 yard line, first down. Less than a minute.

Could Chaparral hold? The Firebirds were not noted for their tough defense in the past. If they could hold Centennial here it would make a big difference in the confidence level that the defensive team needed.

First down. Sweep right. No gain.

Time out to stop the clock.

Second down. The Centennial QB, Mike Strack, dropped straight back and threw a fade to his right–the same pattern that they had scored on earlier over Willden. This time, Matt Willden had perfect position. He had the ball in his hands, but he dropped it.

Third down. The QB decided that he would try Larry Zak on his left, but Larry broke up a quick post pattern in the end zone. Great play.

Fourth down. 10 seconds left. Both stands had been on their feet during the drive by Centennial.

If Jake hadn't blocked that field goal in the second quarter, and they had made it, the score would have been 28-25, and with the ball on the 10 yard line it would have been a "chip shot" field goal. But Jake's big play had taken away that option. And now it was the last play of the game and they had to go for a touchdown.

Fourth down. The QB took the ball from center, rolled to his right looking for a receiver. Everyone was covered. He kept running right toward the sideline. He spotted a receiver, but just as he was about to throw, a speeding Matt Way from his linebacker spot broke through and hit him. The ball fluttered helplessly to the ground and out of bounds.

The defense had held. Pandemonium reigned in the stands, on the sidelines and on the field as the players jumped and hugged each other jubilantly.

They had held! The defense had held! What a great win...the defense had held.

But they didn't know at the time what was awaiting them next week at Greenway, when they again would be severely tested.

CHAPTER FIVE

"DEFENSE COMES OF AGE"

The Saturday morning after the Centennial game, Coach Estabrook wrote on the blackboard, "The Good and the Bad." There was no "ugly" this week.

We had learned a lot about ourselves. We could run the ball—in fact "pound" would be a better word. We could pound the ball against a much bigger line and big linebackers. Also, our defense had the poise, courage and mental toughness to make a game saving stop. And we learned that our passing game needed a lot of work.

Ron Estabrook talked with Scott Johnson on Monday before practice, and found out that Scott had another unnamed person coaching him. Ron told him, "Well, you can't have two coaches. If that's what you want, go ahead. But it won't work." Ron had a very difficult situation to deal with and it took weeks before it was finally resolved. But obviously he had lost confidence in his quarterback. Cobb was moved back to running back.

In the Centennial game, the offense had rushed for 353 yards with Schwartzberg gaining 287 yards for an amazing 13 yards per carry. Griffin had only 41 yards on 10 carries, but he scored twice on the counter, after the fake to Jerry on *33 belly*.

On defense, even though there were two long passes which hurt us, the pass defense had allowed only 8 completions in 23 attempts. And Mike Reisner, 14 tackle points, Chris Dobbins, 12 tackle points, and David Williams with 10 tackle points had led the way on defense. Larry Zak and Matt Willden would play nine more games before they got beat deep again.

Coach Zupke, after looking at the film of Greenway in their win over Arcadia and their loss to Cactus did not think that Greenway would give us much trouble since Cactus had beaten them pretty convincingly, 28-14. A lesson that all coaches have to learn, it seems, over and over again, each year, is not to take comparative scores seriously. And we were about to learn that lesson as Greenway gave us a scare that we would not easily forget. We were all guilty of over-confidence this week.

Matt Way, who would religiously watch our upcoming opponent's film before practice each day of the week, was concerned. Greenway was big. Really big. They had two tackles who were both 6'5" and 280 pounds. Their line looked like a college line, and they had a quarterback, Justin Echol, number 10, who could really throw the football. Their small running back was fast and quick and very tough to bring down in the open field. John Armijo, number 14, was the best tailback that we would see all year.

Chaparral had played at Greenway two years earlier and before the game the Greenway coach had shown Ron his weight room. Ron had said it was by far the most sophisticated that he had ever seen. And after their line had moved our linemen like so many matchsticks, Ron knew that to compete with the Greenway's-of-Arizona-high-school-football, he needed a much better weight training facility than the present one.

The existing weight room was used by the physical education classes and other athletic teams; therefore, it was raggedly maintained. It was easy to point a finger in 360 degrees if things were left out or broken. The weights and weight machines were totally inadequate. To compound the problems, the ceiling was low which made it difficult to do overhead lifts without hitting it. As a result there was no power lifting possible, and only two squat racks for 35 to 40 kids. Ron knew that the weight room was totally inadequate.

Later, he traced the events as they evolved, "When we went to play Greenway in 1995, their coach showed me their new weight facility, and it was beautiful. Their School district had paid for it and the facility was used by their entire school. When Greenway handed my team the worst physical beating that I have ever experienced as a coach, I became painfully aware that we were not on the physical level of other 4-A teams in Arizona."

Chaparral went to Mingus in that same year, 1995, and got physically overpowered– mauled in a game which Ron felt we should have won. After the game he went up to two of his most supportive parents and boosters, Rudy Miller and Jerry Kleven. "I can't compete against the top football programs in the State unless I have adequate weight facilities," he told them.

That conversation was the start of the Chaparral weight program. Rudy and Jerry caught the vision the ball was tossed to them and they didn't fumble it.

The first step was entangled in the question of where to put the weight room: off campus; build a new special building on campus; or fix up the existing weight room?

Ron began to look around the school to see if there were any classrooms, or storage rooms which were not being used. Dr. Kriekard showed Ron a large room which had formerly been used in the metal shop department, but was now being used for storage. It was a mess.

The work began. Ron organized the work parties who cleaned up the room, got it painted, installed mirrors on the wall, and carpet on the floor. There was a core group of eight people who did most of the work. They steam cleaned, power washed, and used a jack hammer to loosen up the fire bricks. It took two dump truck loads to get rid of the debris that had accumulated in that old storeroom.

The Booster Club not only provided the financial support for over $32,000 in new equipment, but donated another $12,000 in labor and material. In less than four months, working every weekend, the weight room was completed.

The contagious wave of enthusiasm eventually spilled over into other areas. Within a nine month period, additional work was completed, repainting the press box, bleachers and scoreboard. The snack bar was renovated, the practice field leveled, seeded and automatic sprinklers were installed. All of these expenses were totally paid off in 1997, under the leadership of Rudy Miller and subsequently, Brian Dobbins, who became President of the Booster Club in 1997.

Once the room and equipment were in place, Ron instituted the BYU weight training program, developed by Chuck Stiggins. Each individual player is tested and then those results are input into the computer, which then prints out a program individually designed for each player.

The first nine weeks emphasizes conditioning with low weight repetitions. The next nine week program shifts more to building strength. The weights become heavier, but there are fewer repetitions. The third nine week period, just prior to August and the start of football practice, is an extremely high-intensity period. After practice begins in August, there is a maintenance phase with lower weights, much like the first nine week period, and instead of Monday, Tuesday, Thursday and Friday, the days during the season shift to Monday, Wednesday and Saturday.

On Monday and Thursday, emphasis is on the body parts—pull lifts, power cleans, and push and press, using the legs to lift, which strengthens the hip, legs and shoulders. There are two different explosions in this particular group of workouts.

On Tuesday and Friday, the emphasis is on speed and anaerobic lifting—squats, leg curls and calf raises, lunges and triceps work.

Wednesdays were the days used for running and agility work. The off-season running program began in late March, in preparation for Spring practice which starts in May. During the summer, Dana Zupke, our weight training and conditioning coach, runs our players three times a week: Mondays; Wednesdays; and Fridays. He also incorporates a couple of 100 yard dashes; 10 - 30's, 10 - 20's and 10 - 10 yard dashes. He also incorporates running over a half-mile for endurance.

• • •

If someone would have told us that we would give up 238 yards rushing and 170 yards passing against Greenway, for a total of 408 yards, and still win the game, we wouldn't have believed them. You just don't give up 408 yards to the other team in total offense and still win, at least not in high school football.

It was Matt Way's first start at linebacker and he was nervous. It had been his dream ever since Pop Warner football to be a starting linebacker at Chaparral, and now his dream was coming true. He knew that to keep the job he would have to perform. David Williams was hurt and this was his chance.

Clay Muschinski and Adam Goodworth remembered two years earlier when the Chaparral line had been out-muscled and out-hit by the Greenway line. Greenway was bigger and much stronger. It was after that game, in the 1996 season, that Coach Estabrook had realized how far behind we were in comparison to the top ranked football programs in the state. Clay and Adam were both looking forward to playing Greenway and measuring how far they had come after two years of intensive weight training. They were both looking for revenge.

Jerry Schwartzberg was again confident that we would win. He also remembered how Greenway had dominated Chaparral two years ago, but he knew that this year's team was a totally different Chaparral team than the one which faced Greenway two years ago.

Jake Ireland, as usual, was ready. He wanted to make a big play against Greenway just as he had against Cactus with a sack, and then with the blocked field goal against Centennial. He was ready.

Greenway started the game by trying an onside kick on the opening kickoff. Chris Medill fell on the ball on our 45. They had an unusual kickoff formation where all of their players would be together in a bunch. They could onside kick it to the middle or outside, pooch it, or kick deep and cover it by spreading out after the kickoff. We had worked hard on this in practice and we were ready for whatever they tried to do.

We only had 55 yards to go for a touchdown, gaining great field position after the onside kick. We just pounded the ball, attacking the right side of their defense, our left, with Jerry scoring on *33 belly*. 6-0. Griffin missed the extra point.

Greenway returned our kickoff to their 35, and then started their own drive with a big play on counter trey for 20 yards.

Trap for 12.

Sweep for 14 yards. Now they were on our 15 yard line.

First down. Incomplete pass thrown in the end zone.

Second down, power over left tackle by Armijo. Three yard gain.

Third down, the quarterback threw a backward pass to the tailback, Armijo, who fumbled it. A loss of 8.

Fourth down. Field goal attempt. The ball is on the 20, so it was a 37 yard attempt. The ball was kicked poorly, and fell short.

In our pre-game warmups, our kickers–Griffin and Cobb–were having problems kicking extra points and field goals because the grass on the Greenway field was so long. I had never seen grass that long–about 4-6 inches long. It made it difficult when the holder put the ball down on the kicking tee, which was sunk underneath the grass.

When the Greenway kicker had been warming up, I watched him carefully to see how he was handling the high grass. He was having the same problems that we were having. I told Coach Estabrook during our pre-game stretching, "No field goals, unless absolutely necessary."

He nodded. We, coaches and players, had noticed and commented on the deep grass. Was it kept long to negate our speed? We didn't have the answer.

So, with the missed field goal we turned them away at the door, so to speak. We would get a lot of practice this night doing that again and again, but there were times when they got through that door.

We took over the ball on our 20, and after one first down, on a run by Jerry on *33 belly* for 12 yards, we couldn't move the ball and we were forced to punt.

Greenway took over on their 32 yard line. And here they came again (on their way to gaining 151 yards rushing in the first half), a trap for 15 yards, and then an interference call on Willden. A trap again for 20 yards by Armijo.

Another off tackle run to our left side, and it was first down on our 7 yard line.

First down. Counter trey right. Loss of one yard.

Second down. QB rolled out right and Jarrad Pavkov, our defensive left end, sacked him for a 10 yard loss. Big play.

Third down. An incomplete pass over the middle.

Fourth down. The QB dropped back to pass and then threw a screen pass to his wide receiver on the right as he broke to the middle, caught the ball and ran behind his blockers, who had let our defensive linemen rush in. But the receiver only made it to the 8 yard line. We had held again. The door was still closed.

This was a huge stop for us because on the next play Jerry took the ball on *33 belly,* broke outside and ran 92 yards down the left sideline for a touchdown. 12-0.

On the extra point, Griffin ran *28 sweep* to his right and scored standing up. 14-0.

On the sideline, as we were getting ready to huddle for the ensuing kickoff, I suggested to Coach Estabrook that we try our middle onside kick. We had been executing it in practice very well, and with the way that Greenway was moving the ball, it might take the wind out of their sails if we could recover it and keep the ball away from their offense, especially their tailback Armijo.

Cobb kicked the ball perfectly, and in the scramble for the ball at the 50 yard line, it rolled down Austin Sendlein's back, hit the ground, and Josh Utterback fell on it.

There was only one problem, though. Jarrad Pavkov, our right end, who was not involved in the play at all, was offside. We had to kick over again. With the element of surprise gone, we kicked deep to the 3, and tackled their returner at their 21.

Very quickly, in eight plays, passing and running, Greenway scored. The extra point was no good. 14-6.

There was 2:54 left in the half. If we could just hold the ball on a drive, and keep their offense from getting the ball, then maybe the defensive coaches could make the necessary adjustments at halftime before any real damage was done.

But Greenway had the momentum now. After 4 plays, we had to punt. Hogue shanked it for only 13 yards. And four plays later, Armijo ran the counter trey to his left side for 35 yards and a touchdown. 14-12. There were 57 seconds left.

On the extra point Greenway took a page from Centennial's book. The QB threw a quick pass over the middle to the tight end, this time to the left. 14-14.

We tried to get a drive together before the half ended. On the first play after the Greenway kickoff, Cobb ran 25 yards on a draw, but after a couple of sacks, a completion, and an incompletion, the half was over.

It was a long walk to our dressing room at Greenway, and the coaching staff was nervous–very nervous. On four Greenway possessions, they had scored twice and gotten inside our 10 yard line twice. We could not stop them. If they didn't score, it was because they stopped themselves.

Our halftimes are all the same. Coach Zupke meets with the defense, along with Coach Heideman and Coach Riccio. Coach Estabrook and the defensive line coach, John Reinhardt, meet with the offensive linemen and the backs. I talk individually with the special teams players, but mostly spend time with the defense and the cornerbacks.

There is no hollering, no emotion–it's very business-like as the coaches talk with the players and make any adjustments that need to be made. Sometimes a team will use a defense that we have not prepared for in practice, and the offensive linemen will have questions about their blocking rules.

But that wasn't the case this day. Dana Zupke had been surprised at how well Greenway had executed their counter trey, where they would pull the guard and the tackle on the same side. The QB will fake the ball to the fullback and he will block any defensive linemen trying to follow the pulling guard and tackle.

The tailback takes a step away from the direction that he is going to run the ball.

It freezes the defense and the little delay gives the guard time to trap the defensive end and time for the tackle running right behind him to pull through the hole created by the pulling guard.

The Washington Redskins, under Joe Gibbs, had been the first team to run this play, and they named it "counter trey."

You know that you are in trouble when your safety is the leading tackler. And Zach Bies, our safety, was making most of the tackles in the first half.

We could not stop counter trey. As the defensive players gathered around Coach Zupke in the locker room, sweat streaming down their faces on this hot September night in Arizona, there was a look of anticipation on their faces. They needed answers. The sweetness of the goal line stand against Centennial was a distant memory. They were in a new battle now, and Coach Zupke had their complete attention.

"Ends, you have gotta' crosshat—come underneath that guard's block—if you don't, and he kicks you out, there's a big hole and their tackle is on our linebacker. Our backs are making all the tackles. You gotta' crosshat." Dana Zupke then demonstrated again the technique. They had worked on it every day in practice.

"Look, when your man blocks down, look for the pulling guard, jam up the hole and make that tailback bounce outside so our linebackers and safetys can make the tackle. You've got to do a better job."

Matt Kelley and Ryan Sydnor were the starters at defensive end, but Adam Goodworth and Jarrad Pavkov also saw a lot of playing time. Dana had been rotating the four of them trying to find the best two who could get the job done.

Dana then talked to the linebackers, "Look, when they are in a one back set, we are in cover four automatically—we're man-to-man. When that setback goes in motion to your side, the linebacker on that side goes with him. You've got him man-to-man. The linebacker away from the motion blitzes. It's automatic—you blitz."

Everyone nodded their heads.

"And linemen, middle linebackers, when you feel a screen coming, stop rushing the passer and look for the screen. We don't need everyone chasing the passer. You can tell when an offensive lineman is letting you in. We need to stop that middle screen to the wide receiver. That's new–we haven't seen them run that before. Be smart. Any questions?"

There were, as the linebackers broke off and met with Coach Heideman, and the defensive backs with me. Greenway was "picking" our cornerback with a back, and that was keeping our cornerbacks from staying with their wide receiver as he cut to the middle of the field along the line of scrimmage. So we talked about that and how to combat it. It was a tough play to defend.

Half-time was over. No pep talks. Just, "Let's go take care of business." It was time for the defense to "come of age."..once and for all.

We had the disadvantage of kicking off to Greenway the second half, and facing that offensive juggernaut again. If we didn't stop them, we were going to be playing catch up. We did not want to be in that position. We wanted to control the ball, and the clock, by running the ball.

Griffin had gotten hurt at the end of the second quarter, so Cobb kicked off to start the second half and kicked it to their 7 yard line. Their returner, behind their wedge, broke it all the way to their 49 yard line. They had gained great field position on their return, which was the last thing that we wanted to see happen on the key defensive series of the game.

After a 5 yard penalty for illegal motion, they ran counter trey. Our end, Matt Kelley, did a good job and they gained just five yards.

Second and 10. Incomplete pass.

Third down. A completed pass over the middle for 21 yards.

First down. Counter trey for only three yards.

Second down. Another illegal motion penalty for five yards.

Second and 12. Bies blitzed, and tackled the QB who was rolling out to his right. Good call by Dana. Loss of 12.

Third down. The QB throws the middle screen to his receiver on the right and Pavkov trips him up, but after he is down, Pavkov makes the mistake of jumping on him. The flag goes down and it is a 15 yard penalty for unnecessary roughness.

Instead of it being 4th and 20, it is now a first down. Pavkov, who was offsides on the onside kick, was capable of making big plays, but he had just made his second mental mistake of the game.

First down. Goodworth replaced Pavkov at left defensive end. The QB rolls out to his right and Goody has him wrapped up for a big loss, but the QB breaks the tackle and completes the pass to one of his receivers at our 7 yard line. Another goal line stand confronted us.

First and goal. Greenway runs counter trey left, but Brad Reisner, our left defensive tackle, breaks through the line and tackles Armijo before he can get started, for a loss of three.

Second and goal. Another motion penalty. The ball is on the 15 yard line now. We've got them going backwards.

Still second down. The tailback goes in motion and Matt Way, the linebacker on the side away from the motion man, blitzes the QB, just as Dana had drawn it up at half time. Against this tough pressure the Greenway QB throws the ball away.

Third and goal. This time the QB drops back 2 steps and throws to his tailback, Armijo, who is behind him running to his right. The QB hits him right in the hands with the ball, but Schwartzberg and Willden come up quickly to force him out of bounds for no gain.

Fourth and goal from the 15. Another field goal. Again, the kicker hits the ball badly, and it is a line drive into the end zone. "The grass is too tall," I say to no one in particular.

Another goal line stand. We did it. The kids are jumping and dancing as they run off the field to the sidelines, where our bench is greeting them with high fives and pats on the back. The war was not over, but we had won the first battle of the second half. You could see the confidence level go up like mercury in a thermometer in July. Their drive had taken almost five minutes and they had nothing to show for it.

Now it was our turn. On first down Ron called a quick slant over the middle to Cobb. We had not been throwing much, and it surprised Greenway. Cobb ran all the way from our 20 to the Greenway 36 yard line for a 44 yard gain.

After a couple of running plays, Scott threw an interception, but on Greenway's first offensive play they fumbled and Willden recovered.

Jerry took a pitchout to his left on *37 pitch* and ran 35 yards for a touchdown.

Cobb kicked the extra point and it was 21-14.

Cobb kicked off to the 5 yard line, and this time our kickoff coverage did the job, tackling the returner on the Greenway 15.

We stopped them on the first two running plays and then on third down Willden made a spectacular play, breaking up a 40 yard pass attempt down the middle.

Fourth down. As it turned out, it was Greenway's only punt of the game. Our punt block team, as they did all season, put tremendous pressure on their punter, and the ball slid off the side of his foot only traveling 19 yards.

First down at Greenway's 39 yard line. Jerry for 6 yards on *33 belly.*

Second down. Jerry for 5 on *31 trap.*

First down. *38 pitch* to Jerry for 5 yards. The quarter ended and we switched ends of the field for what was to be the most explosive fourth quarter of the year–maybe in all of the history of Chaparral football.

Second down. *33 belly* for no gain.

Third down. Ace formation. Jerry is the only set back. Scott drops back to pass–Jerry floats out into the left flat. Scott hits him at the line of scrimmage and Jerry runs down the left sideline, and with a good block by Cobb, Jerry completes the 26 yard run for another touchdown. (He scored 4 TD's for the game.)

Cobb kicked the extra point and it was now 28-14.

There was no collective sigh of relief, or any feeling of satisfaction on our sidelines. Greenway was just too explosive, offensively.

Greenway returned Cobb's kickoff to their 35.

On first down, their QB completed a pass over the middle for 14 yards. They had decided to throw the ball rather than give the ball to Armijo and let him run it.

Second down. Their QB dropped straight back. Three step drop. He threw the ball in the flat to his left, but Matt Way was watching the QB's eyes and read the pass perfectly, jumping in front of the receiver to intercept the ball. He then turned on the after-burners and jetted into the end zone untouched, for a 52 yard touchdown.

Cobb kicked the extra point. It was 35-14.

On the sideline, we were feeling a little better, but we were still not relaxed. There were still a little over 10 minutes to play.

Cobb kicked off to the 3 and it was returned to their 23. Our kickoff coverage was getting better as the game went on.

After a 41 yard pass completion over the middle, the Greenway QB ran a QB draw behind counter trey, blocking to his right. He appeared to have gained 8 yards, but out of a pack of players came number 58, Jake Ireland, with the ball. He ran untouched and almost unnoticed into the end zone before Greenway and our sidelines had any idea what was happening. Big play. Jake had done it again. If we were in kind of a shock at what Jake had done, one can imagine what the Greenway coaches and players must have been feeling.

We missed the extra point, and it was 41-14. But it wasn't over yet.

After returning the kickoff to their 38, Greenway scored in two plays, both *traps*, right up the middle, making it 41-20 as they missed making the two point conversion.

Greenway tried an onside kick, but our left tackle on the kickoff team, Matt Kelley, recovered it on the 50 yard line. After 8 running plays, we were stopped on the Greenway 15.

On first down, the Greenway QB rolled to his right and threw high to his receiver in the flat. The ball bounced off his fingertips into the waiting arms of Zach Bies.

First down on Greenway's 21. Four plays later, Cobb scored on a draw from the 9 yard line, running untouched into the end zone.

Cobb kicked the extra point and it was 48-20.

Greenway scored nine plays later against our second string. Final score 48-28.

In the fourth quarter there had been a total of 6 touchdowns scored by both teams combined. Chaparral had scored 27 points in the quarter, Greenway 14.

Chaparral had run up to 409 yards in total offense and Greenway 408 yards. Even though it had been an offensive show by both teams, Chaparral's defensive stand at the beginning of the third quarter had been the turning point of the game.

And now, the big question for the Firebirds players and coaches was: Could the defense carry over that same defensive intensity for the next game–homecoming against Agua Fria? Had the defense "come of age?"

And then there was that homecoming jinx. Chaparral, as far back as anyone could remember, had never won a homecoming game, and the Chaparral students were letting the football players hear about it. There was a lot of good natured taunting of our football players. The challenge was on!

CHAPTER SIX

"THE DEFENSE'S COMING OUT PARTY"

The Greenway win was a good win for the program. We had gone up against a much bigger team with a great running back, and a good passer, and in the second half had shut down their running game by holding them to 58 yards rushing. In addition, the defense had forced three turnovers in the fourth quarter, two for touchdowns by the linebackers, Jake Ireland and Matt Way.

Zach Bies, our strong safety and just a junior, had an outstanding game making 10 solo tackles and had 22 tackle points. Austin Sendlein, our sophomore linebacker, 6'3" 210 pounds, was fast improving every week, and had 12 tackle points. Mike Reisner, another linebacker had 13 tackle points, and Larry Zak, our right cornerback had 11 tackle points.

Our linebackers were improving every week, and Coach Heideman was drilling them every practice on their reads, filling the correct holes, taking the proper angles, and working on their tackling. He had five linebackers, all of equal ability: Reisner; Sendlein; Ireland; Williams and Way.

Reisner, Ireland and Way also alternated at the offensive guard positions, and David Williams also played at running back, as a backup to Schwartzberg and Cobb. We didn't know it at the time but before the season was over, David would be a very important part of our offense.

Even though the running game had produced its usual numbers—Jerry Schwartzberg for 236 yards on 25 carries for a 9.4 average, and Cobb, 59 yards on 7 carries for an 8.4 average—there was still concern by the coaching staff for the passing game. Scott Johnson had completed 5 for 9 for 113 yards, but the two big gainers to Cobb for 45 yards, and Jerry for 26 yards and a TD, were both 5 yard short passes which they took on the run and made big yardage with, after the catch.

Scott was sacked a couple of times for 24 yards, but that wasn't always his fault as the protection would sometimes break down. But Coach Estabrook had called 12 passing plays, which was more than he had planned. Scott's mechanics were still not correct, and on his interception he had made a poor decision to throw the ball.

In spite of the problem of the passing game, the defense had not been manhandled by the strength of Greenway's line. Our weight training program was paying off.

There were two other significant things, other than the weight program which had happened in the off season. Coach Estabrook was concerned enough with our pass defense that he went to Bruce Snyder, the ASU head coach who had just taken his team to the Rose Bowl. Ron had asked him for help.

Coach Snyder had put Ron and me with his defensive coordinator and defensive backs coach, Phil Snow.

Also, Ron had made some changes in his coaching staff. He had hired Scott Heideman, who had five years of high school coaching, as his linebacker coach, and had moved Dana Zupke, from coaching the linebackers to coaching the defensive ends.

Ron asked me to help him with the defensive backs and to work with him in the passing game. Dennis Riccio, who had just graduated from Eastern Illinois where he had played wide receiver also was hired to work with the receivers and cornerbacks. He was my protege. John Reinhardt, who had been the defensive line coach the past two years, would be Dana's assistant and work specifically with the defensive tackles.

Ron had put together his best coaching staff, one that was competent and dedicated to the same principles that he believed in. Having Scott Heideman come on board was significant, not only because he was a great teacher, but because it allowed Dana to coach the defensive line, which was his strength.

Ron's concern about our pass defense deficiencies in the past year led us to ASU and Phil Snow. We were admirers of Bruce Snyder's program at Arizona State, and we appreciated the time that Coach Snow took to explain not only his defensive philosophy, but also his drills and the techniques that he taught his defensive backs. He gave us a teaching tape on the techniques that his DB's used and we showed it to our kids.

Our DB's learned to back pedal, to read the belt buckle, then the hip pocket, take a quick look at the quarterback and get in the receiver's "ear hole" on man-to-man coverage. We worked on "cushion," that space between receiver and DB, so that our DB's didn't get beat deep. We would give the offense the hitch pass, and the out, but we were determined not to get beat deep.

We installed our pass defense during spring practice so that we would be ready for 7 on 7 passing league games in the summer.

The Firebird's were much improved from the year before, and we were greatly in debt to ASU and their coaches.

In Darren Urban's "Outlook" column on Thursday, the day before the Agua Fria game, he wrote:

> "No one is going to cry for the Firebirds, not after a 3-0 start against some of the best 4A has to offer this season, but quite frankly Chaparral is beat up. More than a couple players have missed practice time this week with bangs and bruises, something that doesn't surprise Coach Ron Estabrook–it's that time of the season.
>
> This game looked like it was going to be a matchup of top 10 teams early in the season, but that's before both Tempe and Mingus carved up the Owl's defense for an average of 52.5 points a game the last two weeks.

There's nothing like unleashing an offense like Chaparral's on a team reeling like that.

But what about Chaparral's defenses, especially when Estabrook raves about Agua Fria's speed? Well, after allowing Greenway to tie the game at 14-14 last week, Estabrook was happy to see an "inspired" performance that basically took the Demons out, including a couple of defensive touchdowns. Injuries? What injuries?

Prediction: Chaparral 45, Agua Fria 14."

Darren had an uncanny knack for predicting winners, and usually came close on the scores.

We also made an important personnel decision this week. It was obvious that Mike Camello, who was very athletic and had a cat-like quickness, was better suited to play corner than safety, where he had started the first three games. He was just not comfortable coming up quickly on run plays. He was too concerned about play action passes.

Matt Willden, our left corner, was a good cover guy, but his strongest asset was his tackling. He was a hard hitter, and along with Bies gave us two hitters who could also cover man-to-man. Both Matt and Camello liked the trade of positions. And it made our defense that much stronger.

Agua Fria kicked off at our Homecoming game under a clear, warm Arizona night. Griffin returned the ball to our 20 yard line. On our first play from scrimmage, *33 belly*, Jerry fumbled at our 18 and Agua Fria recovered. It would be Jerry's last fumble of the year.

Three plays later they scored when their QB threw a short pass over the middle to a receiver and he ran the final 10 yards into the end zone.

They kicked the extra point and it was 7-0, Agua Fria.

Matt Way watched from the sidelines, *"Oh no, not the dreaded homecoming jinx again,"* he told himself. He turned to Adam Goodworth, "No letdown, we aren't going to lose," he told him.

The fumble just made Jerry that much more determined, and he went on to play a game that was probably his best at breaking tackles, as he lowered his head and powered over his tacklers, spinning and running out of the tacklers' arms.

The kickoff by Agua Fria went out of bounds, and we started on our own 35. After nine plays, of which four had been passes, we were forced to punt. Hogue got a 40 yarder off and with a penalty against Agua Fria on the return, Agua Fria started at their own 11 yard line.

Our defense, with Brad Reisner and Chris Dobbins at the tackles and Jake, Mike Reisner and Matt Way, at linebacker stuffed their offense and forced them to punt.

It was short, and we took over on their 40. On first down, with Jerry dragging tacklers, he picked up 12 yards on *33 belly*.

On the next play, Griffin took a pitch on 27 and ran, untouched, 28 yards for a touchdown.

As usual, on all long runs John Hogue, our wide receiver, would have a key block. Griffin kicked the extra point. 7-7.

On Agua Fria's next possession, after a first down, Jake got the QB on a sack for an 11 yard loss and then a couple of plays later Matt Kelley recovered a fumble.

Six plays later, Chaparral scored again as Jerry ran it up the middle from the one. The two big plays on the drive had been a run by Griffin on *24 counter*, and a pass from Scott to Cobb on *belly pass*.

The Firebirds forced Agua Fria to punt after five plays and took over on their own 10. It took seven plays this time to go 90 yards with Griffin scoring again on *24 counter* from 31 yards away. Again, he just outran the defenders with his tremendous quickness and speed.

Kick was good. 21-7.

Chaparral shut down their offense again on the next possession. Four and out.

Cobb caught the punt on his 35 yard line, started up the middle, looked like he was going to head for the left sideline. Suddenly, remembering that we were setting up a wall on the right sideline, he cut sharply to his right and then headed down the sideline all the way to the Agua Fria 25 before being pushed out of bounds. A 40 yard punt return.

But after two running plays and two incompleted passes, Agua Fria took over on downs.

On the last play of the half, Larry Zak picked off a pass by the halfback on a fake run.

Agua Fria returned the second half kickoff to their 38. Our defense stuffed Agua Fria on the first two downs and on third down they completed a hitch-pass to one of their receivers, who then fumbled. Josh Utterback recovered for us.

Starting on our 44, it took eight plays to score with Jerry gaining 41 yards of that on *31 trap*, which he ran three times. Jerry scored on *34 belly* from 13 yards out. On the play before, with the ball on their 18, the defensive tackle lined up opposite Clay Muschinski, jumped offside, and leveled Clay, knocking him to the ground head-over-heels. As Clay would say later, "Even though it was a penalty, it was really embarrassing. I made up my mind to decleat him on the next play." And he did. Revenge was sweet. 28-7.

Agua Fria started their next series on their 28, after the kick-off. The defense again held on three downs with Jake and Bies getting great hits on their tackles.

This time on fourth down the snap from center was a little high and the punter had to jump for it. When he came down he saw, coming from his right, Hogue and Pavkov bearing down on him. He quickly decided not to punt, but after running a few steps to his right, Hogue and Pavkov trapped him at the Agua Fria 15 yard line.

For the second time in the game the special teams had given the ball to the offense inside the opponent's 30 yard line.

Four plays later, Griffin scored on *27 pitch* from 7 yards out, making a great cut back inside a couple of blocks. 35-7. Cobb later scored from the one yard line. Final score, 42-7.

Our kids were relieved. They could finally go to the Homecoming Dance on Saturday night and hold their heads high. They'd managed to break the Homecoming Jinx which had haunted the Chaparral team for years.

The defense, with the ends cross hatting their pulling guards, the tackles getting penetration and pursuing, and the linebackers filling, was devastating. Chaparral shut down Agua Fria's rushing game, allowing only 31 yards rushing and minus 20 in the second half. Coach Zupke said that the ends were tired of cross hatting in practice all week. But it worked, he had them ready.

The offense had rushed for 318 yards with Schwartzberg gaining 142 yards on 22 carries for a 6.5 average. Agua Fria had obviously set their offense to stop Jerry, which was way below his average, although respectable. With Agua Fria keying on Jerry, it had allowed the two halfbacks to gain a lot of yardage. Josh Griffin gained 114 yards on 10 carries for an 11.4 average, and Ryan Cobb gained 43 yards on three carries for a 14.3 average. Cobb also had one pass reception for 55 yards, and a punt return for 40 yards.

On defense, Jake had 16 tackle points and a fumble recovery, by far his best day. Way was next with 8. After that, it was pretty well even among the rest of the team.

As Coach Estabrook was quoted later in The Tribune column by Darren Urban, "We had a saying all week, that this was the week for our 'defense's coming-out party', and I think they did."

There wasn't much celebrating after the game or the next day. We all knew what was ahead–Flagstaff High School, inside the Dome at NAU, at an elevation of 7,500 feet. It was the most intimidating place in all of Arizona to play a high school football team, and on top of that they just beat up on Saguaro 49-37.

CHAPTER SEVEN

"CONQUERING THE DOME–FLAGSTAFF"

Coach Ron Estabrook was concerned with the mental adjustment of our kids, who were going to play in an indoor football stadium and on astro-turf. There was the additional problem of playing at an elevation of 7,500 feet above sea level. Coach Zupke, however, was having more mundane concerns, such as stopping #12, Mack Jones.

The week before, against Saguaro, in their 49-33 win, Flagstaff had turned Jones loose for 239 yards and five touchdowns. This was Jerry Schwartzberg type stats. In addition, Jones had thrown to a wide receiver for a 19 yard touchdown pass on a fake sweep.

Dana had started working the past week on a new technique with the defensive ends. He was drilling them on "reading" the downblock of either the offensive tackle or tight end, whichever one was on their side.

This week was going to be an important week for our defensive ends, Matt Kelley, Ryan Sydnor, Jarrad Pavkov and Adam Goodworth. Dana's plan was to shut down the off tackle hole and try to bounce Jones outside where our linebackers and safetys would be waiting for him. Flagstaffs offense was based around a typical pro I formation, but Jones was bigger than most high school pro I tailbacks. He was big, 6'2", 200 pounds, and extremely fast.

Matt Way was excited about this game against Flagstaff High School. To play at NAU in a domed stadium which seated 15,000 was a major event in his life. It was a big deal. He made the statement, "I'm not worried about the long drive making us tired, or the elevation, I just want to play in that domed stadium." Matt knew that "Flag" had a huge line after watching film on them all week, but he felt that our line was better, and that Flagstaff was just an average team standing in our way of going 5-0.

Jerry Schwartzberg didn't know what to expect. The last long trip that we had taken to Mingus two years ago, in the 1995 season, had ended poorly. We were not ready to play and Mingus had beaten us by three touchdowns.

"We need to prove that we can play relentless-type football on long road games," he told the others.

He was concerned that the team would be intimidated by the high altitude. He had heard that the Flagstaff newspaper had picked the home team to beat us. Jerry smiled to himself. He loved being the underdog–loved the challenge.

Jake Ireland was worried about Mack Jones, his great speed and athletic ability, and he was also a little intimidated by the domed stadium.

Clay Muschinski and Adam Goodworth both felt that this game was the most important game of the season. Could we overcome the elevation, the Dome, astro-turf, and Mack Jones?

Coach Estabrook had come to Flagstaff with the Chaparral football team back in 1994 to help Gary Mauldin, in the booth on the phones upstairs, during the game. He had remembered how awed the kids were when they walked in the Dome, straight off the bus, after a three and a half hour ride. Flagstaff had scored three quick first quarter touchdowns before our kids got over the whole intimidation experience. The rest of that game had been pretty evenly played.

Ron was determined that this year's game would not be a repeat of 1994. He was familiar with indoor stadiums, having played in three championship games at UNLV in Las Vegas, Nevada.

The surface of the field was the practical problem. What shoes do you wear? Cleats used outdoors are not feasible on indoor astroturf. Ron had each player bring two or three pairs of shoes that they could try on and run in before the game. Adam Goodworth wore his beloved army boots, which he would sometimes wear on our outdoor practice field.

To cut down on the intimidation factor, Ron called the NAU coaching staff and asked if we could visit the Dome early in the afternoon after we had our late lunch. (Normally teams weren't allowed into the Dome until just before the game.) This would give the kids time to throw the ball around, try out their shoes, and get comfortable with the "feel"of the Dome. It was different. It's hard to explain, except to say that this whole experience is different from what we normally do on Friday nights.

The game starting time was even different, starting at 7:30 rather than 7:00 o'clock–no big deal; however, just one more domino on an already unbalanced stack.

To combat the elevation factor, Ron decided to have the bus leave early Friday morning so that the kids would have time to adjust to the unusually high altitude. Ron wasn't sure of the practical benefits, but he thought that mentally it would be a big help to the kids. Whether there is any scientific proof to back that up we really didn't know. All we knew was that the kids never mentioned being winded after the game started.

This was also a big game for our linebacker coach, Scott Heideman. He had played at Flagstaff on their State Championship team in 1983, and the present coach, Coach Holland, had been his coach. His family and friends would be at the game and he was proud of the way that his linebackers had been playing. He wanted to show them off for his former coach and friends.

There was also an interesting sidelight to the football game. As the team was trying out their shoes, and getting used to the Dome, I noticed the NAU basketball team walk out from the weight room. They sat down on a bench, watching us warm up. (Their team made it to the NCAA tournament in 1998 after winning their conference.)

I went over to talk with them and in the course of the conversation found out that they were waiting for us to finish working out so that they could start their running–a part of their pre-season training program.

One of the players asked me, "Where is your group from?"

I told him, "Chaparral High School."

He tightened the laces on his shoes, "That's where Brad Snyder was from," he told me.

"That's right. What a shame he was killed. I used to watch his dad, Dick Snyder, play in Charlotte, N.C., when he played for Davidson, back in the mid-sixties." (Dick was an All American and later played in the NBA.)

His son, Brad, had played at Chaparral a few years back and was an All State basketball player in Arizona. He had a sweet jump shot. After a game one night, when he was playing for NAU, he left Flagstaff to drive to Phoenix to see his girlfriend. Not far from Flagstaff, he swerved to miss a deer, hit a median and was thrown from his vehicle–killed instantly. He was a great kid and his loss was deeply felt in the Scottsdale Community.

Brad's parents, Dick and Terie, had formed a scholarship fund at Chaparral. Dick went on a bike-a-thon from Seattle to Virginia, biking 140 miles per day, to raise money for the fund. They also formed a "Head Smart" program in the Scottsdale elementary district aimed at preventing head injuries. They still conduct an annual golf tournament in Brad's memory to help contribute to the fund. Great people have a way of turning tragedy into victory.

The basketball player and I most likely would never talk again. But we had shared a moment of remembrance of a great athlete and the difference his short life had made in the world.

I turned my attention back to the kids, who seemed to be thawing out their awe of the Dome.

Coach Estabrook was still concerned about his passing game. The running game had turned the Firebirds into an offensive powerhouse. After four games, Schwartzberg had gained 877 yards on 97 attempts for an average of 9.0 yards per carry, and he had scored 8 TD's.

Griffin had gained 316 yards on 38 carries for an 8.3 average and had also scored 8 TD's. Cobb, whose numbers would increase dramatically after this next game, had gained 120 yards on 15 carries for an 8.0 average, and 2 TD's. He also had four catches for 119 yards and a 29.8 average per catch.

Flagstaff was another one of our opponents who had an offensive line that was much bigger than our own. They had little fast backs on defense, but what Ron didn't have any way of knowing before the opening kickoff, was that this would be his team's best offensive game of the year.

Chaparral took the opening kickoff and, in eight precision-like plays, scored when Cobb ran off left tackle on *45 power* for 11 yards. Griffin had a 22 yard run on *28 sweep* when he broke a couple of tackles, and Jerry had two runs of 15 and 10 yards.

The touchdown on our first series helped the mental attitude on the sidelines. There was still much apprehension though. On Flagstaff's first possession Zach Bies intercepted a pass on the far sideline right in front of the Flagstaff bench. The ball was on their 33 yard line.

On our first play from scrimmage, Griffin took a handoff from Scott going to his right. It looked like *26 power*, except that after a couple of steps, Griffin made an inside handoff to Cobb, going from right to left.

We call it *45 crisscross*: Cobb cuts up inside the right guard, Jake Ireland, who has pulled to his left, kicking the end out. Our tight end, Adam Goodworth pulls through the hole and blocks the linebacker, and John Hogue, our wide receiver, runs downfield and blocks the defensive back. Cobb ran the ball for 30 yards to the 3.

On the next play Griffin ran *28 sweep* for a TD.

Our sideline was noisy, as were our fans behind us. The noise level was magnified inside the enclosed Dome. The excitement didn't last very long as the Flagstaff kickoff returner caught Griffin's kick on the 10 yard line, started up the middle, cut to his right and was off on a 90 yard TD run. It took the wind out of our sails momentarily.

It was now Chaparral 13, Flagstaff 7.

On our next possession, Scott threw a perfect pass to Griffin down the left sidelines for what could have been a TD, but Griffin dropped it, and Hogue had to punt. He got off a good punt to the Flagstaff 11, where Williams, Way and Ireland dropped the returner in his tracks.

After a first down, Flagstaff was forced to punt. The punt block team put such pressure on the punter that the ball went straight up in the air and bounced out of bounds on their 31. It was an 8 yard punt.

But we didn't put the ball in the end zone. After four plays, Flagstaff took over. It was the last time that Chaparral would be stopped all night. The Firebirds would score on their next six possessions.

Griffin scored the third TD of the game on *26 crisscross* (just the opposite of *45 crisscross*), and he broke a couple of tackles as he scampered for 56 yards.

On the fourth TD, 53 seconds before the first half ended, Scott threw a five yard "out pattern" to his right to Cobb, and Cobb sprinted the final 37 yards to complete a 42 yard TD. The first drive of the second half, Flagstaff got on the board again with a 10 yard run for a TD by Mack Jones, but that would not have happened if Jake had not roughed the passer on fourth down. It did not look like a good call to us. Their drive took six minutes off the clock. 26-13.

On the ensuing kickoff, Jerry ran a reverse back to our 42, and then five plays later he ran *32 trap*, cut back to his left and scored from 30 yards away. 33-13. You could see the air go out on the Flagstaff sideline.

On their third play from scrimmage, Zach Bies recovered a fumble, and six plays later Cobb scored again on *45 criss cross* from 16 yards away. 39-13.

The next touchdown came after a great defensive play on third down by Matt Way, who "smelled out" a screen pass on third down.

Matt's time spent on watching film helped him anticipate the screen pass, and he tackled the Flag back for a two yard loss.

Again, the punt block team almost blocked the punt and the pressure forced the punter into a 10 yard punt. Our punt block team, led by David Williams, was relentless.

Six plays later, Griffin ran a draw the final 11 yards for the TD. 45-13.

Pavkov recovered our pooch kickoff and Chris Medill scored the final TD on *45 power,* running 24 yards for the TD.

Final Score was 52-20. They scored against our second string in the final minutes.

We had 10 offensive possessions, punted once, got stopped on fourth down once, and scored the other eight times.

The Flagstaff punter, who had made the All State team the year before, punted four times for a 14.3 average, which was due to the pressure of our punt block team.

Jerry had 166 yards in 21 carries for a 7.9 average and a TD. Griffin had gained 118 yards on just 11 carries for a 10.7 average, and 3 TD's. Cobb had gained 88 yards on 10 carries for an 8.8 average. He had caught a TD pass for 42 yards, and had a total of three TD's for the night. Scott was 3 for 6 and 82 yards, and a TD pass.

The defense played another outstanding game, creating four turnovers. Willden, our safety, had an interception and 14 tackle points with seven individual tackles. Chris Dobbins, our defensive tackle was all over the place with his quick pursuit and had 9 points. The defense had held Flag's powerful running game to 123 yards and shut down the dangerous Mack Jones. The Firebird pass defense played tough all night, allowing short completion and gave up only 59 yards on 10 completions in 19 attempts.

The most astounding statistic was the offensive production– 495 total offensive yards.

There was a good feeling of accomplishment on the long bus ride home. But on the next day, after the Flag film session, Coach Estabrook laid it out for the players. It was a sobering message.

"All right, we're 5-0 in our non-conference games. Now comes the big test. We now start our second season–the five conference games, and then our third season, the playoff games be-gin. We haven't beaten Coronado in three years. We need to win this game."

The expressions on the kid's faces changed radically. There was a new look of determination as they began to realize that a new challenge now awaited them.

"Coronado is the most important game of the year. They're going to be tough. They're always tough. We've got a big week ahead of us."

It was going to be a vigorous challenge for the coaches too. Playing against a Joe Corte coached team was always tough.

CHAPTER EIGHT

"CORONADO–JOE CORTE AND JOEL HUERTA"

The Chaparral seniors had remembered Joel Huerta from the past two years. He had killed us with long runs in the Coronado 12-10 win of 1995, and had gained 212 yards against us in 1996, in a 34-28 Coronado win. Our kids were totally focused on stopping #25, Joel Huerta.

The Firebird's coaching staff was just as concerned about Huerta, but more so about Joe Corte, the long time head coach at Coronado, and his coaching staff. Year-after-year they made the playoffs with usually the smallest team in the State. But they made up for their lack of size with toughness. They were fundamentally sound on blocking and tackling, made few mistakes, and always had one or two great running backs. The Coronado "Dons" were perpetually one of the best coached teams in the State.

Joe Corte always had a good game plan for us and the Chaparral coaches had many discussions trying to figure out what they thought Joe would try to do against us this year.

•   •   •

105

After the season was over, Joe Corte related to me what his week was like, Chaparral week for Coronado.

Meanwhile, on the Saturday morning the week before Chaparral and Coronado were scheduled to play, Joe Corte and his assistant coaches strategized at Coronado. They reviewed the films of Chaparral's win over Flagstaff. They also scrutinized videos from the two previous games–Agua Fria and Greenway.

Joe hit the off button on the VCR. "You know, Chaparral's linemen have always had good technique, but they didn't seem to have the strength to move people when they blocked. This year they're stronger–a lot stronger." He frowned.

He was rightfully concerned. This year's Coronado linemen were not as big and not as strong as his previous teams. He needed to find a way to neutralize Chaparral's line. As he and his assistant coaches rolled up their sleeves and developed their game plan over that weekend, Joe became increasingly convinced that the biggest priority for the Coronado "Dons" was to stop Jerry Schwartzberg. He was strong with great quickness, and he was hard to bring down when he got into the open field–he just broke tackles.

Coach Corte was willing to concede Griffin and Cobb their yards–they were fast and ran to the outside on sweeps very well. If Nick Poole could play at linebacker, it would be a big help, but if Nick didn't recover from his injury, Coronado could be in big trouble. The backup for Nick was very small, and Joe needed someone who could match up with Schwartzberg and be able to tackle him in the open field.

He verbalized the looming question to his assistants, "If we stop Jerry, will they throw? Chaparral hasn't passed much this year. I went back in my files and dug out Chaparral's pass patterns from past years. This is a much better team than the year before."

There were nods of agreement around the table.

"They're much better defensively." He had watched Chaparral's freshman and junior varsity teams play on Thursday against his teams the past couple of years, and he could see that Chaparral now had a program.

"All of the teams ran the same plays, same defense, same special teams, and the kids are getting faster, quicker, stronger, and bigger–their weight training program is beginning to catch up with Coronado's."

He stood and stretched out the kinks from sitting for a length of time. "Here's the offensive game plan: We're going to throw short." Their excellent passer, and receiver, J.D Durbin, would lend their skills to this strategy.

"If we throw short passes on Chaparral's cornerbacks, who seem to be 'deep conscious', it should throw them off balance. They seem concerned about allowing long passes."

Smiles began to break over the assistant coaches faces as they sensed the wisdom of this game plan.

"We'll throw deep every now and then just to keep it honest," he gestured broadly with one hand and laughed.

The other key move he disclosed to his coaches was to switch the fullback, Joel Huerta, to a halfback position when he wanted to get outside with the sweep. "This tactic won't show up anywhere in the past, so Chaparral won't be able to see it on tape and key on it. I'm mostly concerned with Chaparral's linebackers. They line up six yards deep and come on hard–aggressively."

The game was to be played on a Thursday night rather than Friday, due to the fact that sundown Friday would be the start of the Jewish holiday, Yom Kipper. John Kriekard, the Chaparral principal, was being sensitive to that.

Darren Urban's pro-game column in <u>The Tribune</u> was written on Wednesday this week:

> "Records: Coronado 3-2, Chaparral 5-0.
> Outlook: Ah, the beginning of the region schedule. It signals the start of the stretch run to the playoffs and brings together (at least in the East Sky Region) the city teams.
>
> <u>And can there be a better game to kick it off than this one?</u>

Midway through the season, Chaparral has proven to be every bit as good as expected, beating back some pretty decent teams by grounding out a lot of yards, passing at key moments and playing a level of defense unheard of in a couple of years at the school. Despite Tempe's early success (and the Buffaloes are the real deal), the Firebirds have to be the favorite to win the region.

The Dons, most likely, will need an upset win over either Chaparral or Tempe to make it into the postseason again, and that's assuming Coronado wins its other three region outings. In the end, 7-3 can make the playoffs; 6-4 will not.

The way both teams have been playing, and with the backfield talent available (see: Schwartzberg, Griffin, Huerta) this very well could end up being a fast-moving game. Coronado receiver J.D. Durbin could be an 'X' factor that aids the Dons, who will need extra help against loaded Chaparral.

Another small twist: The last time there was a big upset in the East Sky the first week of the region schedule, Chaparral shocked big favorite Tempe two years ago, and the Firebirds went on to win the region. Something to think about for both sides tonight.

Prediction: Chaparral 35, Coronado 21."

The night of October 10 was muggy and warm as Joe Corte gathered his players together in the visitors' locker room at Chaparral, just minutes before the opening kickoff. He had decided to use an excerpt from Mel Gibson's pre-battle speech in the movie, *BRAVEHEART*. His words resounded off the metal lockers and walls of the room.

"All right, men! We're going to lift our kilts, show 'em what we've got, and charge!"

The Coronado players went crazy, jumping up and down, screaming, and fighting their way out the locker room door. Joe's motto was, "Respect everybody, fear nobody."

The stage was set for a rugged battle of the "brave hearts."

The opening kickoff by Coronado went to the Chaparral 37, where Chris Medill fell on it.

Coach Corte respected Chaparral's kicking game–he actually wished that he had the kickers that Chaparral had; therefore, he wasn't about to kick it deep where "the big three"–Griffin, Cobb and Schwartzberg were waiting for the ball. He had remembered two years earlier when Jerry had taken a handoff on a reverse, in a memorable kickoff return, and had gone all the way for a touchdown. He had made up his mind never to kick the ball deep again to Chaparral and had not done so the previous year either.

Joe's fears about Jerry were realized when on the first play from scrimmage, on the Chaparral 37, Jerry took the handoff from Scott on *32 trap*, up the middle behind Mike Reisner's trap block, he knocked over the linebacker, cut back behind Griffin's block, and then broke to his left behind Cobb's and Hogue's blocks downfield. He ran the ball all the way to Coronado's 10 yard line before being tackled.

The Coronado sideline was silent as the explosive run by Jerry seemed to slow the charge and dampened their initial enthusiasm.

On the next play, Griffin, out of the double tight formation, took the handoff from Scott, and running to his right behind the blocking of the right side of the line, and Reisner's and Jerry's block, scored easily on *26 power.* 7-0.

Cobb was now kicking the extra points for us. We had decided that Griffin had enough to do, so we took that responsibility from him. Griffin would still kick off until Scott Lane came up from the junior varsity later in the season. We were blessed with three kickers: Cobb; Griffin; and Lane. The three had worked all year, starting in January, kicking on Sunday mornings in Charlie Gorham's and my kicking camp. Griffin kicked off to Coronado and with good coverage we tackled their returner on the 20 yard line. We were kicking the ball away from #25, Joel Huerta, and to their number 33.

On the second play after the kickoff, Ryan Sydnor recovered a Coronado fumble at their 25 yard line. Four plays later, Griffin took the ball on the 9 yard line on *26 power* and ran it to the 1 yard line, where he was forced out of bounds. But there was a clip on the play, and now we were on our 22.

On a play action pass, we had another penalty, this time for holding.

On fourth down from the 33, Scott decided to run it, rather than pass. He made it to the Coronado 19 yard line.

So, after eight plays that started at the 25, we had had two penalties for 25 yards, and three pass plays called with no completions. Coach Estabrook would call only one more pass play for the rest of the game.

On Coronado's next offensive series, our defense held, but on fourth down our punt block team roughed their punter, which gave them a new lease on life and a first down.

In sixteen plays, they covered 82 yards, taking seven minutes off the clock. 7-7.

On Coronado's kickoff, Michael Camello picked up the bouncing ball at the 30 and ran it back to our 39.

On the first play, Coach Estabrook tried the same play, *32 trap*, that he had run on the first play of the game. Jerry ran 61 yards for a touchdown, again with good blocking from the offensive line, and Hogue, Griffin and Cobb making blocks downfield. 14-7.

On Coronado's next possession, the defense held, shutting Huerta down.

On fourth down, David Williams jumped over the punt protector and blocked the punt. It was a spectacular play! Davey had kept his eyes on the ball even as he was being blocked. The ball rolled into the end zone and Larry Zak fell on it for a TD. 21-7. The Chaparral sideline erupted . There is nothing like a blocked punt for a TD to spark excitement.

Starting on their 22, after the ensuing kickoff, the Coronado Dons started to drive, mixing up their plays with short passes and draw plays to Huerta.

Durbin made a spectacular catch, taking the ball out of Camello's hands, and landed on our 3 yard line.

Three plays later, Huerta scored and it was 21-14.

The half ended. In an unbelievable statistical reversal, Chaparral had the ball for only 12 plays, while Coronado had 33 first half plays. Jerry's two long runs, and the blocked punt by Williams contributed to the first half story for Chaparral.

When the Firebirds kicked off to start the second half, the defense was very aware of how important the first series was. If Coronado was to take the ball and score, tie the game up, it was going to be a real dogfight. And Joel Huerta had the potential of breaking a long run at any time.

The first series was a big one for the defense. And they stepped up.

First down, Huerta ran off tackle to his left. Chris Dobbins, Matt Kelley and Matt Way did their job and gang-tackled Huerta before he could get started. A two yard loss.

Second down. Huerta up the middle for 5 yards.

Third down. The Coronado QB rolled to his left and was sacked by Jake, Dobbins and Brad Reisner for a 3 yard loss.

Fourth down. The punt only travelled 28 yards as the punter hurried to get the punt off. Blocked punts have that effect on punters.

Now it was the Chaparral offense's turn. They needed to put together a drive and put this game out of reach. Ron Estabrook had decided at halftime to pound the ball inside, just like the second half of the Centennial game.

First down. *33 belly* for 4 yards.

Second down. *34 belly* for 5 yards.

Third and 1. *33 belly* for 5 yards.

First down. *32 trap* for 1 yard.

Second down. *34 belly* for 4 yards.

Coronado's defensive line and linebackers were making it tough to break a long play. They were digging in.

Third down. After five straight running plays by Jerry, Ron called a fake on *32 trap* and a give to Griffin on *28 sweep* which went for 7 yards.

First down. Coach Estabrook called *28 waggle*, but again Scott didn't throw the ball, and took a 6 yard loss.

Second down and 16. Scott faked to Jerry on *34 belly,* and handed the ball off to Cobb, who ran behind Elle Davis' trap block on *43 counter.* Cobb blasted for 17 yards to the Coronado 19.

On the next play, Jerry ran *32 trap* behind Mike Reisner's block, cut to his left and literally ran over the Coronado cornerback on his way into the end zone. 28-14.

On our next kickoff, we made the mistake of kicking the ball to Huerta and he returned it from his 5 yard line to his 37. We were lucky that he didn't break it all the way.

Mike Reisner forced the QB to intentionally ground the ball on first down, and after two more downs of going nowhere, Coronado had to punt.

Chaparral took over on its own 37. After ten plays, on *33 belly*, Goody, our tight end blocked down on their end, who was on a "stunt" trying to close the off-tackle hole. Jerry bounced it outside, powered over one tackler, ran through the arms of another and ran 26 yards for the TD. 35-14.

On Coronado's next possession, with the aid of an interference call, they scored after 10 plays on a QB sneak from the 1 yard line.

It took Chaparral three plays to score on its next possession. Griffin ran *28 sweep*, breaking a couple of tackles, for 19 yards, and then Cobb ran *47 sweep* for 36 yards to the 2 yard line. Jerry bulled his way over on 31. 42-21. Final score.

Joe Corte's concern about Jerry Schwartzberg was right on the money, as Jerry gained 212 yards on 20 carries for a 10.6 yard average per carry and four touchdowns.

Cobb had 77 yards on eight carries for a 9.6 yard average. Griffin, on only seven carries, had picked up 49 yards for a 7.0 yard average. Chaparral's running game had picked up 345 yards, while holding Coronado to 169 yards rushing.

We had zero yards passing.

Joel Huerta had gained 129 yards in 29 carries for a 4.4 average, almost two yards below his average. The Chaparral defense had risen to the occasion and kept Huerta from breaking any long runs. The Coronado passing game was effective, 8 for 11 for 78 yards, but 35 of those yards were on Durbin's spectacular catch.

112

Matt Way had a great game at linebacker with 19 points, the high for the year, of any defensive player. Zach Bies had 16, Chris Dobbins 13, Jake Ireland 12, Mike Reisner 10, and Matt Willden 9. Adam Goodworth, only playing about half of the game on defense, had 8.

As the Firebirds began intense preparation for their next opponent, Apache Junction, they were naively unaware of the disaster which awaited them on the following Friday night.

CHAPTER NINE

"GOOD NEWS: A PASSING GAME
AND BAD NEWS: A DISASTER STRIKES"

On Monday, there were disturbing signs that this would not be a good week. The Scottsdale School District had instituted a new policy this year–there would be a week off from school–a mini break in October. And on that Monday of no school, we had four players who didn't show up for practice.

Just before practice started, Cindy Muschinski, Clay's mother, called and said that Clay, Adam Goodworth and Ryan Sydnor had gone to San Diego for the weekend. They had decided on Monday to have Clay's older brother, Corbin, show them around the University of San Diego. Because of this, they would take a later plane back to Phoenix and would miss practice.

Cindy had called so that they would have an "excused" practice rather than "unexcused." "Excused" meant that they would play in the Apache Junction game, but they would not start. Had Cindy not called, it would have been an "unexcused" practice and they would not have been permitted to play at all.

The fourth player, Jarrad Pavkov, had also gone to California. He went to visit family living there. Jarrad took the first three days off and then showed up on Thursday. He had not called to explain his absence. Coach Estabrook had already gone the second, third and fourth mile with Jarrad, who had missed at least one practice per week.

Jarrad, who was a big play-type of player, had played well on special teams and at defensive end, but he had not communicated with Coach Estabrook where he was this week.

When Ron saw him, he made it short and bittersweet, "Jarrad, the talking is over. Turn in your equipment to Leon."

Leon Sturtz, our equipment manager, took Jarrad's equipment reluctantly. He really liked the boy as all of us did. He watched Jarrad as he slowly left the field, his shoulders drooping, head bowed. He knew what the rules were, and even though he had the ability to be an important part of the team, Jarrod never seemed to make the commitment Ron demanded and expected.

Matt Way took it harder perhaps than the rest. He told me later, "I took Jarrod to practice the day after he came back from Callifornia. He asked me if Coach would be mad, and I told him not to worry about it. Then later, during that practice I couldn't find him in the defensive groups. I asked someone where he was and found out Coach had kicked him off the team. Boy, did I feel lousy about telling him not to worry about it."

Earlier, that same Monday afternoon in the coaches' office, Ron had received a telephone call from Scott Johnson's father, Chuck Johnson. In the course of the conversation, Chuck had conveyed that Scott had been very upset with his role in the previous game. Even though four pass plays had been called, he had officially only thrown one pass for 0 yards. Only one of those pass plays had been called in the second half. Over the weekend Scott had expressed his frustration to his father, who in turn called Ron on Monday afternoon.

Ron responded from the basis of previous clearly defined principles, "Chuck, you know my policy, if a player has a problem with any one of the coaches, he comes to see me first. If we can't work it out, then he can bring his parents into the discussion, and Chuck, Scott hasn't come to me, and until he does, I don't think this conversation should take place."

Chuck Johnson persisted and wouldn't conclude the discussion by deferring it to Scott, so that he and his coach could talk about it. From the viewpoint of many a coach, they sometimes fantasized about charging parents with imaginary penalties for "interference." However, there is another side to that penalty flag: parent's just naturally want what is best for their sons; it is almost an anomalous act to let go and step back rather than tackle anybody who is suspected of violating the rights of their special child. It takes a unique patience to cope with parents in a sport which engenders emotion anyway.

Chuck Johnson continued to pursue the subject and would not hang up. He persisted in letting Ron know what he thought of him, "If you're a quarterback coach, I'm a brain surgeon!" he announced hotly.

Ron frowned, bit his lip and told him, "I've got to get to practice. I'm going to hang up now."

Chuck Johnson had been critical of Ron and his game strategy to other parents in the stands on Friday night. These parents had related the comments to Ron, but there was nothing that Ron could do about it but take it in stride. Chuck Johnson's words could possibly act as a pernicious infection to the morale of the parents, coach and ultimately the team. Team unity was a fragile thing and Ron did not want a parent to upset the delicate balance that he had worked so hard to develop.

Coaches are very sensitive to the chemistry of a team, especially if there are players who have a big ego and an inflated sense of self-worth. Football is the ultimate team game. No matter how good a running back is, he needs to have an offensive line blocking effectively in order for him to be successful.

Jerry Schwartzberg was an excellent example of one who understood this principle. He would always show appreciation to his offensive line by giving them his "birdies." After reviewing the game films on Saturday mornings, the coaches would reward players for their effort from the night before with "birdies," which stood for a shortening of the word "Firebirds." This was actually a sticker in the form of a football which was pasted onto the helmet and awarded for best hits, fumble recoveries, sacks, best catch, best blocks, "mister hustle," and best offensive, defensive and special teams players. Also, if the defense and special teams met their goals, those teams got birdies, in addition to a birdie for each game that was won.

Our kids wore these symbols on their helmets with glowing pride, similar to World War II pilots, who painted hash marks on their fighter planes for the number of enemy fighters shot down.

Therefore, when Jerry gave those sticker trophies awarded to him, to his offensive linemen, it symbolized a gesture of ultimate appreciation for their efforts which helped him. It cemented the ideal of team endeavor.

Both Jerry and Jake Ireland had been concerned about team chemistry before the season started, in particular at San Diego State during the first week of pre-season practice. Each season the team would take off for San Diego for the first week of practice in August. First, it got us out of the Arizona heat, which usually was 110 degrees in the afternoon, and secondly it helped to develop team bonding and team chemistry. The players and coaches lived together for five days in one of the dormitories on campus. There were two practices a day and then meetings at night.

At the meeting on the first night in San Diego, Ron decided it might be a nice time to announce to the team that the Booster Club planned to pay for the first pre-game meal of the season. They had chosen Emily's Restaurant, located about two blocks from our school to host this special event. This was the first year that Coach Estabrook had arranged for the team to eat together, then assemble in the weight room in order to get ready mentally to play, before going to the locker room to dress.

In the past the players had gone home, or maybe to a fast food restaurant to eat. Ron was aware that there were even some players who did not eat at all. He was confident that all the players would be enthusiastic about his plan–feel appreciative for this type of support and thoughtfulness from the Booster Club.

But just to make sure, he asked for a show of hands of those players who liked the idea. Almost all of the hands went up, except for four–Scott Johnson and Clay Muschinski were two of the dissenters. Later that evening after that meeting, Scott and Clay had another team meeting in their room. They wanted to go home after school, eat at home, and then come back to school when it was time to get dressed. Jerry and Jake both told everyone they liked the Coach's plan, and thought it would help team bonding. Both sides laid out their arguments in a friendly manner, but the players listening had now become evenly divided. It had become a "big deal" and there seemed to be no resolution until Adam Goodworth appeared at the door, late for their meeting.

The minute Adam sat down, Jerry pounced on the opportunity to get his input. "I think that the team pre-game meal will help build togetherness, and team spirit. What do you think?"

Adam thought a moment. "Sounds good to me," he responded.

Someone sitting on the floor got up and said, "Well, that's it." The meeting was over as the room emptied.

Adam was not one of the captains, but he was so well respected that when he said something it carried a lot of weight.

Team unity was still intact.

•   •   •

Now, as Ron hurried toward the practice field after his disconcerting telephone call from Scott's father, he thought back over the team cohesiveness from their time together in San Diego. He realized he was not as steamed at the telephone conversation as he'd thought he would be.

It was an injustice to Scott, however, to overlook the importance of Scott coming directly to his coach. *After all, one of the highest values of the sport is grooming our kids not just to become great athletes, but well rounded young men.* He could see the players warming up in the distance as he walked swiftly toward them. *They are young men–they need to learn the importance of standing up for themselves, overcoming their own battles.*

There had been tension between the Johnsons and Coach Estabrook for two years. Scott, who held most of the school's passing records and had thrown for 1484 yards and 17 touchdowns in his junior season, was expecting another big season this year.

He had thrown well in the 16 summer passing league games, although sometimes his mechanics seemed to be off kilter.

Perhaps a measure of the tension stemmed from the fact that Chuck had wanted Ron to hire an assistant coach whose specialty was coaching quarterbacks and the passing game. There had even been a luncheon meeting with Ron prior to the season to communicate his thoughts on the Chaparral passing game.

Ron did not normally meet with parents in this manner, but consented because of the very obvious tension which had developed between him and Scott's parents.

In the previous 1996 season, Chuck Johnson had been critical of Ron's coaching from the stands during games and afterward. His remarks had filtered back to Ron; however, he made it a point to never respond to second guessing and criticism which was non-constructive.

During this period he told me that he thought of himself as "only an adequate quarterback coach." I disagreed with him and with Chuck Johnson's assessment.

I had coached quarterbacks in high school, and two of them, who had terrible techniques before I worked with them in fine-tuning skills, later went on to college and set passing records.

Billy King broke a number of Ivy League passing records at Dartmouth, including my brother, Jim Mottley's, at Princeton. Whitey Lipscomb had broken a number of small college passing records at Hampden Sydney College in the state of Virginia.

My brother, Jim, had set a couple of passing records while he played at Princeton, and he had assisted me at St. Christopher's one year by bringing a set of passing drills from Princeton which were helpful in the development of a passing game.

I had told all that to Ron the year prior when I felt he wasn't giving himself enough credit as a good quarterback coach–I had watched him work with them for three years. Ron was good. It wasn't just a back-slapping session, I wanted him to know I had the credentials to judge his true worth.

I also verbalized to him that I disagreed with Chuck Johnson's parental approach. I had also been a parent of a player, just a few years earlier. My son, Jed, had played wide receiver and cornerback at Chaparral a few years prior.

During that period, I would go to practices and watch, not just to watch Jed exclusively, but sit there and enjoy the things which go on in practice...things only a former coach could appreciate.

There was a vicarious thrill to watching the linemen in their one-on-one blocking drills, or the receivers as they challenged the defensive backs. And yes, I saw things I would have done differently (before the days of Ron Estabrook)–not that what the coaches were doing was wrong; I just might have instructed differently. However, not once did I ever try to coach my son or tell him to do something different than what his coaches were telling him. I would not have wanted fathers doing that to me when I was coaching.

Perhaps of even greater importance, is the burden it puts on the player–he becomes a victim of being pulled in two directions– trying to please two masters. I suspected many times when Scott chose to not throw the ball, it was because his mental decision seesawed between the sideline and the stands. This is unfair pressure.

I remembered one game in which Jed played as upback (sometimes referred to as "fullback") on the kickoff receive team. He was lined up on the 25 yard line. The ball was kicked just over his head. He dropped back about six or seven yards, caught the ball and began to run with it.

Chuck Johnson was sitting next to me. His other son, Brian, was on that team. He turned to me at the time and said, "Why don't you tell Jed not to drop back like that?"

It would never occur to me to have told Jed whether he should catch a ball kicked just over his head. I was not his coach. He already had a coach and he needed to do whatever his coach asked of him, not what I asked.

Conversely, now that I have that responsibility at Chaparral, I coach our upbacks not to take more than one step back if the ball comes their way. If it's over their heads we want the deep returners to catch it. They are already running at full speed. So actually

121

Chuck Johnson's assessment was correct–his approach was what I disagreed with.

At the time, I turned to him and remarked, "Having been a coach, I think that I appreciate the relationship between players and coaches more than most fathers." I wished I had said more but confined it to just those words.

For the past three seasons Chuck had been video taping his son, Scott's, offense from the stands in passing league and then in the regular season games. This, in itself, could have just been the actions of a proud father wanting to record his son's performance for posterity; however, Ron suspected the tape was used as a tool to dissect Scott's errors and the receiver's and blocker's errors. It became increasingly obvious that Scott Johnson had more than one coach.

The results of dueling coaches began to manifest itself in the earlier part of the season when Scott's mechanics were not good. He seemed unsure of himself, and no wonder. Ron perceived Scott's obvious reluctance to throw the ball under pressure, and therefore take the sack, was a direct result of two sets of instructions hitting his mind. Even when the receiver was covered, Ron insisted that Scott throw the ball away, "up in the stands, somewhere! But don't take the sack–it's killing our drives," Ron told him.

The Tuesday afternoon prior to the Apache Junction game, the day after his phone conversation with Chuck Johnson, Ron took Scott into the football office before practice. It was time to talk–even though it hadn't been initiated by Scott.

He seemed uncomfortable. Surely he knew his father had called the Coach.

Ron was serious–hit the problem head-on. "The way we're going is not working."

Scott nodded his head in agreement.

"You've had your own coaching, and I've tried to adjust to that instead of fighting it. Now, I think you'd agree, we need to do something...get off dead center here. It's affecting your performance–our games." It was important to handle this delicately–

not denigrate or diminish Scott's relationship with his father in any way.

Scott nodded again, but Ron saw a flicker of something undefinable in his eyes.

"I now know that we've got a good team. We can go deep into the playoffs, but we can't do it unless we throw the ball effectively. You and I are going to work together to get this job done. We both need to concentrate on this for the good of the team."

Another nod. So far, Scott hadn't said a word.

"You are going to have to do it my way. If you do, I will commit to you that I am going to take the wraps off our passing game—we'll throw the ball from now on."

"Okay," Scott said.

"Here's what I'm going to do. First of all, during defensive group drills I'm going to let Coach Mottley take the safeties with him so that I can work exclusively with you on your mechanics during that period. Bob Kuch sent me a tape on quarterback mechanics that we'll look at together. We're going to start over—go back to basics, Scott. Then, during the offensive group period I'm going to work with you and the receivers. I'm bringing Coach Heideman up from working with the line so that he can coach the running backs. That will leave me free to work with you."

Bob Kuch had helped Ron in developing his passing game. Although our basic offense is the Wing -T, there are actually five different offensive formations. The Chaparral passing game is very sophisticated and Bob Kuch had used a lot of the so called "West Coast" passing philosophy employed by Bill Walsh of the Forty-Niners.

Scott nodded again. He smiled. "I'll do my best," he said.

"My commitment to you is twofold: I'm going to spend more time with you; and I'm committing to you that I'm going to throw the ball from now on. One more thing, Scott, we're going to work on short, timing passing routes. The only time that we'll throw long is when I "tag it." ("tag it" means that instead of throwing the ball to the primary receiver, that Ron would pre-determine a secondary receiver, usually a pass to a receiver who was running a deep route).

They headed for the practice field together. Ron had a feeling of relief about their talk. Scott was certainly deserving of the extra attention–his latent skills were excellent–and he felt that the conversation had not impinged, or negatively reflected on the relationship Scott had with his father. This practice week would be key for the Chaparral football team. For them to be successful, they had to develop a passing game.

This week was important to Ron Estabrook for an additional reason. For the first time this year, Chaparral was playing a team they should beat, handily. And Ron was interested to see if his team would keep the same level of intensity that it had all year. He was concerned that over-confidence could hurt that level of intensity. Not having Goodworth, Muschinski and Sydnor at practice on Monday set warning bells off. Ron had already decided that afternoon what he was going to have to do about Pavkov.

•   •   •

The team gathered around Dana Zupke in the surroundings of their own locker room just before game time. It was another hot October night in Arizona. Apache Junction had not had a good football team in a number of years and in the past two years had not won a game. This year, however, under a new coach who had done an outstanding job, the Prospectors of Apache Junction were digging in. They were 3 and 3.

The Firebirds were definitely "up" for the game. The locker room resounded with slamming metal doors, the sound of cleats on tile, and good natured shouts back and forth. Shoulder pads were adjusted, a broken shoe lace replaced, and in the hallway outside of the locker room, the team gathered around for the pre-game talk. Coach Dana Zupke looked at each team member singularly. The buzz of conversations died quickly as he waited for silence.

"Tonight we play a much improved Apache Junction team. They have been winning...they have a new attitude...they're on the right track."

He made eye contact around the room. "Sometimes, however, when you're on the right track, you get knocked off by the train coming through."

There were a few wrinkled foreheads–quizzical expressions.

"We are that train! And they are on *our track!"*

Smiles broke out everywhere.

"Sure, they are doing better and we must take them seriously, but they are in our way. They're trying to keep us from our destiny!"

As further realization broke over them there were shouts of "Yeah!"

"They cannot play with us, they have no business on our field!"

Dana had an "amen corner" now. The kids were with him and vocalized it.

"We will show them that by: out blocking, out tackling, out executing, and out hitting them. They cannot have what we have! They must get off our track or get run over!"

More shouts of agreement.

"Because the Firebird train is coming through, and we're going to blow up anything that gets in our way!!! War on 3! One, Two, Three," he shouted.

The team responded as one, "War!" they screamed.

Talk about lighting a fire...Dana detonated a bomb under the team. They exploded out the door and headed for the field in a cloud of war whoops and yells.

On Apache Junction's opening kickoff the ball went out of bounds, which was a penalty, and Chaparral took over on their own 35 yard line.

First down. Scott took a three step drop and hit John Hogue with a six yard hitch pass. Hogue turned upfield for another five yards, before being tackled on our 46.

On the next play, Scott faked the ball to Jerry on *33 belly* and rolled to his left to pass. His receivers were covered and instead of being sacked, he tucked the ball away and ran straight ahead, lowering his shoulder on the tackler for a gain of four yards.

I looked over at Ron; he was clapping his hands like a gleeful small child. Dana hollered, "Yeah!" over top of Scott Heideman's "Yes!" I found myself clapping and saying silently to myself, "Go for it, Scott, this is *your* game."

Second and 6. Griffin took off on *28 sweep* for 31 yards before being pushed out of bounds. But there was a clip on the play, and the ball was brought all the way back to our 38.

On the next play, Scott faked to Jerry, then to Griffin on *28 waggle* and found Jerry open in the left flat for 11 yards. It wasn't enough for a first down; Hogue had to punt.

The Firebird defense shut Apache Junction down and forced them to punt.

Chaparral started this drive on their own 16 yard line. It took 12 plays to cover the 84 yards for a touchdown. There had been four pass plays called. Griffin had dropped one, Scott had run on another pass play for 16 yards, and the other two had been completed to Cobb for a total of 25 yards. Griffin finished the drive off from the 10 yard line, overpowering two would be tacklers. 7-0.

The defense again held the Prospectors and forced them to punt. Chaparral took over on their own 17. This time it took seven plays to go 73 yards, the big plays being *27 pitch* to Griffin for 17 yards, a seven yard pass to Cobb, and a touchdown pass down the left sideline to Griffin on an out and up pattern for 33 yards. 14-0.

The defense again stopped the Prospectors on their own 49 yard line, forcing them to punt.

Instead of punting the ball, their punter threw a long pass to his right end who was streaking down the field, but Michael Camello played it perfectly. He reached up and grabbed the ball away from the Apache Junction player on the Chaparral 35 yard line. He then ran it back 41 yards down his left sideline before he was tackled on the Apache Junction 24 yard line.

Five plays later, with the ball on the 11 yard line, Scott sprinted to his left, set up, and found Griffin all alone in the end zone for a TD. 21-0.

Knowing glances were exchanged between the coaches. We had been together long enough now to read each other's thoughts well. The time spent with Scott had paid off.

Again, the defense held Apache Junction and forced them to punt. This time the ball rolled out of bounds on their 44. Now, there were under two minutes left in the half.

First down, Scott hit Austin Sendlein, the big sophomore tight end, who had replaced Goodworth, on *28 waggle* for 16 yards.

After a penalty, Scott hit Cobb on a 5 yard out, and Cobb sprinted all the way to the 10 yard line before he was pushed out of bounds on the right sideline.

Two plays later, with seven seconds left on the clock, Scott took a three step drop, looked to his right and threw a TD pass to Hogue, who made a nice catch on a slant pattern with a defender sprawled all over him. 28-0.

Seven seconds left in the half and Griffin kicked off. The first person downfield on the coverage looked like he was shot out of a cannon he was running so fast. His number was even a blur. He grabbed at the ballcarrier with his left arm, but was going so fast he couldn't plant his feet and make the tackle. The next tackler down, Austin Sendlein made the tackle at the 21 yard line.

The player who had missed the tackle was still lying on the ground writhing in pain. Suddenly we realized it was Jerry Schwartzberg. The stadium became eerily quiet as Coach Estabrook, the trainer David McAdon, and Dr. Dicke ran onto the field.

I held my breath as I reflected that it had been an unusual night for Jerry. He had carried the ball nine times for only 48 yards and a 5.3 yard average per carry. He had not broken any long runs like he usually did. The Apache Junction defense was set to stop him, and that had allowed Scott to throw the ball for three touchdowns in the first half.

Later, Jerry shared his thoughts. He was frustrated with his lack of production. On the extra point attempt, just before this kickoff, Jerry had been lined up on the left wing, a yard behind the left end, and he attacked the defender as the ball was snapped, driving him into the end zone. He knew his job was to wait, and not let any defender get through him and the tight end, not attack him. The frustration had continued on the kickoff. When we get a couple of touchdowns ahead, Jerry is supposed to let his backup, Jeff O'Connell, take his place. As Jeff started toward the huddle, however, Jerry waved him off and trotted out to take his position.

Now, as Jerry lay on the ground with Dr. Dicke's fingers probing the area around his right knee, he fought back hot tears which singed his cheeks. He perceived that something really serious had happened. He had heard and felt a snap when he tried to stop as he was reaching for the Apache Junction returner.

The world seemed to be turning upside down as he lay on the ground. He had always felt invincible...the strongest player on the team...he'd worked hard to be in the best possible physical condition. How could this be happening to him? He found strong arms lifting him upward. As he limped off the field, supported by the trainer and Dr. Dicke, there was sustained applause. Jake Ireland, his best friend, looked pained as though he too experienced an injury of his own.

In the locker room, at halftime, Dr. Dicke examined him further. He shook his head, "You've got to get an MRI on Monday, Jerry. I don't think anything's broken, but I believe you've torn the ACL."

Jerry's eyebrows raised. "What's that?"

"The Anterior Cruciate ligament in your right knee. It's going to take some time to mend."

"No! No!" Jake vocalized the feelings of the players who had gathered around.

I patted Jerry on the shoulder. I looked around at the rest of the kids. It was obvious that the consequence of Jerry's injury had slowly begun to impact them with the additional burden this would now place on them. Could they overcome this overwhelming setback? Could Jerry overcome the pain and frustration?

The second half of the game was an anti-climax to the emotions which had swirled in the locker room at halftime.

Cobb and Griffin made a couple of good runs, and Cobb had scored, but the TD was called back on a penalty. And then Cobb kicked a 40 yard field goal. Apache Junction scored a TD with six minutes to go. The final score was 31-6.

Scott had a great night completing 14 for 19 passes for three touchdowns. He also ran for 18 yards on two carries. Ron's conversation with Scott, his very positive approach with Scott, had obviously been the right one. Scott was confident and he showed it.

Griffin had 71 yards on eight carries for an 8.9 average, and two TD's. Cobb had 61 yards on eight carries for a 7.6 average. David Williams, who filled in for Jerry in the second half, had 34 yards in 5 carries for a 6.8 yard average.

The offense now had more balance with the running game picking up 241 yards and the passing game had 175 yards for a total of 418 total yards of offense.

The defense had put on quite a show holding the Prospectors to 77 yards rushing and 52 passing on 7 for 17. Matt Way again led the way with 12 tackle points, Mike Reisner and Matt Willden each had 11, and Matt Kelley had 10.

But the second half was played with a different intensity than the first half. Jerry's injury was on everybody's mind. All of the coaches seemed to feel as dazed as I was. It was hard to concentrate on the game going on in front of us. Griffin, who never fumbled, had his only fumble of the year in the second half. And our sideline enthusiasm was as low as I've ever seen a winning sideline be.

Adam Goodworth and Clay Muschinski had not played the first half as a result of their practice absence. Clay said later, "I was up for not playing the first half, and it was really a different experience after three years of always being out there. Actually, I was surprised how much fun it was to watch the team and cheer them on...but Jerry's injury was awful to watch."

Adam said he also had enjoyed watching, but after the game in the locker room, Adam sat down beside Clay. They hadn't changed out of their uniforms yet. They sat silently mulling over Jerry's injury. The silence was finally broken by Adam, "Clay, it's time to rock and roll!"

"Yeah, we've now got to prove we're not a one man team."

With one hand, Adam wiped a small river of sweat off his forehead, sprinkling the floor with it. "And we're playing Saguaro next week. We've got to get ready."

Saguaro High School, located just a couple of miles away, had turned their season around since they had lost to Flagstaff. They had upset Tempe and then beaten Arcadia. But it would not have made any difference if Saguaro had not even won a single game as Chaparral and Saguaro were bitter rivals–too bitter. Some of the players on each team had played together and against each other on Pop Warner teams for years.

This game would have been the toughest game of the year even with Jerry. Now that he would not be playing, there was a certain apprehension, a stealthy self-doubt, which crept into the consciousness of the Chaparral players. And even though we didn't want to admit it, the coaches felt it too.

The game was to be played at Saguaro which added to the discomfort. Could the team possibly rise above losing one of their Captains and their key player? Would morale plummet as a re-sult–performance tailspin? None of us could have known at the time that it was to be the most exciting game of the year...

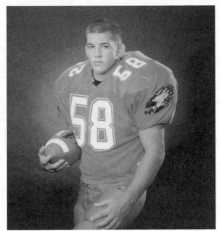

Jake Ireland

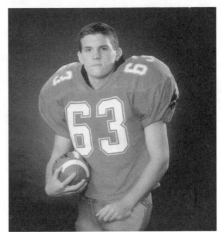

Matt Way

Adam Goodworth

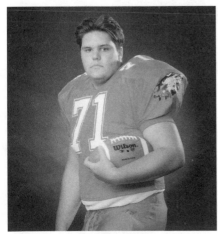

Clay Muschinski

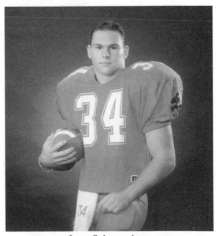

Jerry Schwartzberg

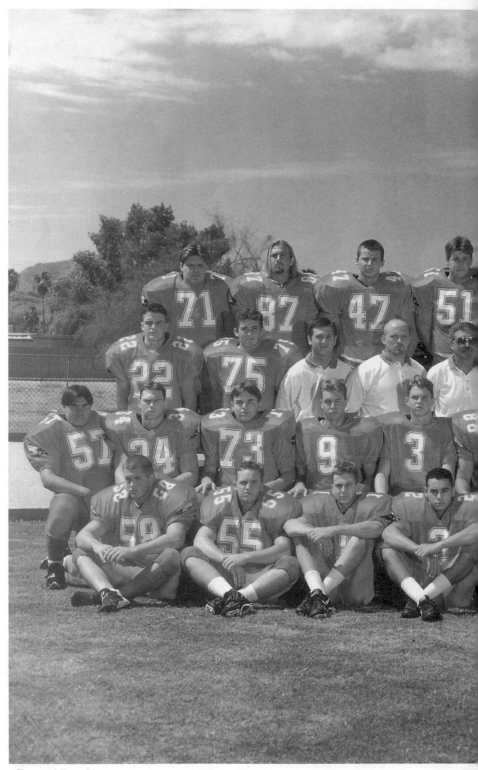

Chaparral Team Picture

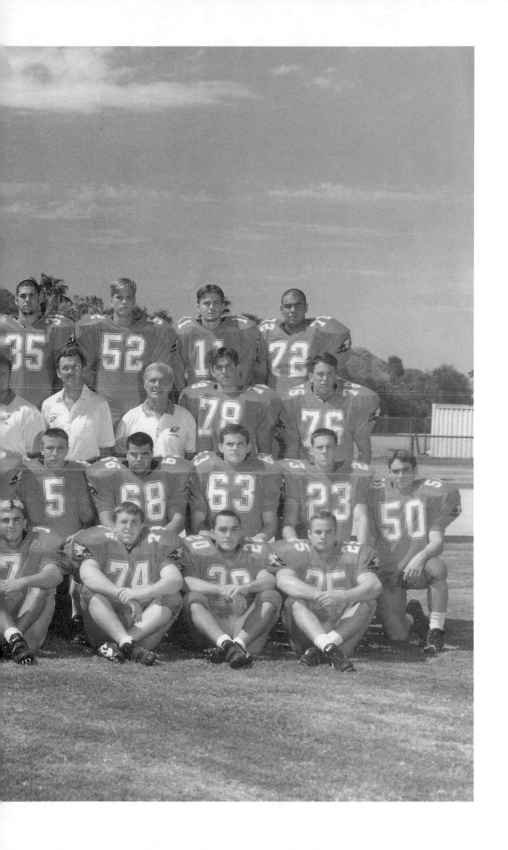

Chaparral Boosters after a game

Coach Mottley, Matt Willden, Ryan Cobb

Red Caughron

Coach Mottley and wife, Linda

Coach Reinhardt and Family

Quarterback Scott Johnson

Coach Mottley, Coach Estabrook,
Principal John Kriekard

Kickers: Scott Lane, John Hogue,
Ryan Cobb, Josh Griffin

Linebackers: Mike Reisner, Jake Ireland, Austin Sendlein, Matt Way, David Williams

Josh Griffin breaking a tackle against Cactus

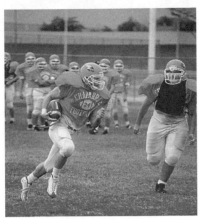

David Williams, Coach Zupke, Austin Sendlein

Chaparral practice

Jerry Schwartzberg at practice

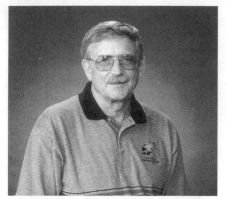

Coach Estabrook

Coach Zupke

Coach Heideman

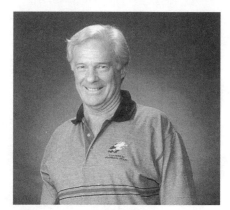

Coach Mottley

Chaparral Seniors under the scoreboard after the Saguard playoff game

CHAPTER TEN

"THE COMEBACK KIDS"

During the week prior to the Saguaro game, the Chaparral coaches tried to casually sound out the kids. The bitter rivalry which existed between our two teams warranted taking the emotional blood pressure of members of the team. Compounding the ingredient of high rivalry, Jerry's injury tended to undermine confidence for the coming game; therefore, we felt it important to get a baseline of feelings, take the temperature of the guys to see if the team felt the goalposts had been moved.

Jake Ireland admitted his best friend's injury was a devastating personal blow. In fact, he revealed he was being assaulted by thoughts of not wanting to play anymore. It was as though they had been joined at the hip in working out, taking trips to each of the ten schools they would play during the season in their jinx-spell grass snipping capers.

In addition to concerns about Jerry's injury, Jake indicated he had been disappointed he hadn't started at middle linebacker. Coach Heideman had been pleased with the way that his big sophomore middle linebacker, Austin Sendlein, had been improving. By having Austin start at middle linebacker, it meant Jake could now just play right guard on offense, and only have to go one way. Jake was still going to play defense, but this would keep him fresher by not having to play both positions. Mike Reisner, the "ironman," was now the only player going both ways, at left offensive guard and left linebacker.

Jake and Coach Heideman had an excellent working relationship; however, the summer before when Coach Heideman was new to the team it had seemed to the kids that he was rigidly demanding. Slowly, they began to learn that he also had a great sense of humor.

Once Jake saw the humorous side of Coach Heideman's personality, he tried to appeal to that. At the time, he didn't know that the Coach's humor was deeply buried during serious drills.

The linebackers were lined up for a drill and Coach Heideman told them, "When you see me folding my arms over an imaginary ball, that means it's a run...you should charge forward. When I stick my chest out and raise my hands, it means that it's a pass and you should drop into your zone."

Jake, thinking a little humor might relax everybody said, "Coach, your chest is so small, stick it out real far so we can see it."

Matt Way started laughing.

"Way," Coach Heideman's voice commanded in a no-nonsense tone, "why are you laughing?"

"'Cause of what Jake said, Coach," came the reply.

Scott Heideman leveled them with an indignant look. "Okay, both you guys hit the ground and start doing push ups."

It was an object lesson for both kids. They learned there is a place for humor–Coach Heideman displayed it readily at other times–but not during drills.

•   •   •

Matt Way seemed to be revved up and champing at the bit to play. Saguaro was the game he looked forward to the most. This would be the first time he had played against Saguaro since they had previously been in another conference. They had been moved from 5A to 4A. Matt admitted he was apprehensive, especially as it would be the first game in three years he had played without Jerry.

There were other signs of portent. Scuddling gray clouds and distant lightening had hovered over the practice field threatening rain on other occasions. Jerry had always seemed to shake a mental fist at them declaring, "It's not going to rain. We need the practice—we're going to play at ASU in the championship game. Strangely enough, it had never rained during practice..."not in three years straight!"

The Monday after Jerry's injury, however, it poured as though the heavens had opened up on us. In fact, I thought perhaps Ron might call off the practice because of the heavy deluge. Most of the kids came up to me later and commented that Jerry's absence had allowed it to rain.

Coach Estabrook told the team after practice on Monday that Jerry would most likely be out for the season. He stressed that everybody would just have to "step up." It was pointed out that the Firebirds were not a one-man team, and that everyone could count on David Williams to get the job done. Matt said he took Coach's statements to heart. He knew Saguaro's line was a lot bigger than ours, and that their "horse," Andrew Brigham, was a powerful runner pounding the ball from tackle-to-tackle. Brigham was 6'3", 220 pounds and an excellent athlete. It would be key to stop him at the line of scrimmage before he got into the open field.

Matt knew if we beat Saguaro it would mean that Chaparral would win the Region Championship. The game, therefore, had weightier significance that just being a bitter rivalry. Matt watched film all week and was convinced Chaparral was quicker and smarter. He told us he had every confidence that David Williams would be "a great replacement for Jerry."

Adam Goodworth had a rivalry going of a more personal nature. His brother, Craig, had played end on Saguaro's State Championship team two years prior. The brothers had always been highly competitive, and Adam wanted to wear a championship ring of his own, too.

He vowed to play harder, hustle every play, make every block and hopefully the ball would be thrown to him a lot so he could score a touchdown on every reception. Adam's face reddened as he told me, "I've never been as fired up for a game as I am for this one."

Clay Machinski had seen film on Brad Selby. He was a virtual Freeway retaining wall at 6'7", 280 pounds, but Clay personally felt he was a better offensive lineman. In spite of all the glowing press Selby had received, Clay secretly believed he was a better blocker. He knew he'd have to step up his game, but he considered the game Friday night to be a stage where the coaches, press and student body would make the startling comparison between him and Selby.

Jerry Schwartzberg mentally wrestled alligators. He told us, "I know it's not this big a deal, but it's like my life is starting all over again." He had run the emotional gauntlet of "not really believing it was happening to him," to feeling "a low like I've never felt before. I find myself wanting to run and hide—never be found again." He smiled and adjusted the height of one crutch. "But that's not me." This was punctuated by a slightly self-conscious smile.

Jerry confided he'd been holding pep talks with himself. "I can beat the unbeatable, I can do it. I'll come back faster than anyone else has ever done. I'll be ready in three weeks, not six weeks." Apparently it was like a mantra. Jerry seemed to love a challenge even if it was against time and nature.

There hadn't been much swelling. The doctors were encouraging, suggesting that if his rehab went well, there was a chance he could be back in time to play in the second or third playoff games. His determination would have matched that of a disgruntled bear running in the forest who just plows through anything which gets in his way. He told us he considered it "another test, and I will overcome this and play in the State Championship game," as if to speak the words would make them materialize. His affirmations seemed to be welded in a mind-set hammered from iron. I only hoped the future didn't hold further disappointment.

Sometimes goals which are set too high get dashed on the rocks of circumstances.

. . .

Meanwhile, Walt Sword, the Saguaro head football coach, geared up for the game with the Firebirds. At practice on Monday he told his team, "Forget about what the newspapers are saying about Schwartzberg. We're going to prepare for this game as if he's going to play."

Coach Sword's plan of approaching the injury issue of Jerry was sound. If Jerry did play, there would be no letdown, no emotional fallout. If he didn't play, it should pump up his team.

As he prepared his team for the game Friday night, he told me much later that he had decided they would run the ball first, establish the running game, then throw the ball. Walt had made a change in his coaching staff after the Flagstaff game. His young offensive coordinator was not following his instructions and his game plan of controlling the ball longer on offense by running Brigham more. He had a big horse in Brigham, and by running him he could control the clock and rest his defense by keeping them off the field while the offense had the ball.

Walt, frustrated by his assistant coach's insistence of doing things his own way, had to let him go in the middle of the season. Embarrassing as it had been, it had been the right decision. Brigham, who had only been carrying the ball eight times a game, was now running the ball twenty-five times a game. As a result, Saguaro was controlling the ball, plus the clock, and had pulled a big upset by beating unbeaten Tempe. Tempe had beaten the number one ranked team in the State, Peoria, and had tied Mingus.

Walt wasn't giving up on his passing game. He had an excellent quarterback in Ryan Dobson. In my interview with him after the season, he said all he wanted was a more balanced attack–that was his game plan against Chaparral. He had been working on an unbalanced line with a wingback lined up between the tackle and end in a slot formation. He was ready to use it against Tempe, but didn't need it. He did plan to use it against us, he revealed in his post mortem conversation with me.

Defensively, Walt made a significant change to combat Chaparral's offense. He had been the defensive coordinator two years prior for the Saguaro State Championship team, and took great pride in his defense. Walt had always run an eight man front, and three deep with his defensive backs normally playing a zone. But with all of Chaparral's motion by their running backs, it was very difficult to cover all of their receivers.

In the summer passing league, Chaparral had hurt his three deep zone pass defense. So he had made a change this week, deploying a seven man front and using four defensive backs instead of three. It gave him greater flexibility, and after seeing how Scott Johnson had destroyed Apache Junction's defense, completing 14 out of 19 for 175 yards, he knew that he would have to respect Chaparral's passing attack.

In Darren Urban's pre-game column in The Tribune he had written:

> "Outlook": This is the game both teams have been looking forward to all season. And fortunately, in the first meeting between the rivals since 1992, the region Championship is in the balance–it really couldn't have been scripted any better.
>
> To listen to the two coaches talk about the game is fun–Saguaro coach, Walt Sword, compares Chaparral to the 1995 Saguaro state champs, while Chaparral coach, Ron Estabrook, raves about Saguaro's size and athletic attributes–it is almost a lesson in downplaying your own teams. But don't be confused, because both coaches are quietly confident in what their teams have accomplished of late.
>
> There is a question, and a very big one, of how Chaparral will perform mentally after the loss of star fullback Jerry Swartzberg with a knee injury. Backup David Williams, welcome to the bright lights of Schwartzberg's world. Josh Griffin (554 yards) and

Ryan Cobb (346) must turn it up and QB Scott Johnson has to produce as he did last week (175 yards, three TD's). Saguaro's big line will get tested by perhaps the best defense it has seen this season, so we'll find out how effective the bruising running game will be. QB Ryan Dobson will need to complete some passes.

The return of the rivalry, a championship as a reward, even properly chilly fall weather as a backdrop. Isn't this how high school football was drawn up?

Prediction: Chaparral 24, Saguaro 21."

Nature set the perfect stage that Friday night. A full moon drifted lazily in the sky regarding the excited throngs of people who jammed into the Saguaro High School stadium. It hovered like half an exclamation point, waiting for the kickoff. The night air was crisp with temperatures in the 50's–unusual for Arizona in the month of October. The wind had come up and was blowing hard from north to south, yet sometimes it swirled about like a forceful woman frivolously changing her mind at the last minute.

Jake Ireland had sat alone on the short bus ride to Saguaro. It was obvious he missed his buddy, Jerry. And during the warmups, he searched the sidelines to see if Jerry was there. But no Jerry.

Later, at the coin toss, he saw him sitting on the bench, all alone, crutches resting against his legs. As Jake moved toward him, Jerry got up, slapped his friend on the back and said firmly, "Go get 'em!"

Jake swallowed hard and turned back toward the field. He looked back one last time, "We're going to win this one for you...do it for you, Jerry!" he pledged.

Saguaro High School had one of the State's most unusual stadiums. The home side stands were made of concrete rather than the usual metal. They were almost twice the height of normal stands as they climbed skyward like an ancient Aztec temple.

The visitor's side stands were constructed of metal. This night, the visitor's stands were packed with Chaparral students, fans and its band. The crowd overflowed into the standing room area beside the stands. Although Saguaro had a big crowd on their side, it looked as though their rivals, the Chaparral Firebirds had an even bigger and certainly more raucous crowd. The noise was deafening from both sides even before the game began.

Mike Rubino, the Saguaro kicker, kicked off. With the swirling wind now behind him, he kicked the ball into the end zone.

First down from the 20 yard line. Scott sprinted out right, found no receiver open, put his head down and ran it for a one yard gain.

Second down. Scott reverse pivoted to his left and handed the ball off to David Williams on *33 belly*. 10 yards–Clay and Adam had moved their men completely off the line of scrimmage, which they would do all night long.

First down. Cobb on *47 sweep*. The line blocked down, and Mike Reisner at left guard pulled to his left and hooked the end. Cobb ran for 8 yards around left end before being tackled by the Saguaro cornerback and safety.

Second down and two. Griffin ran for three yards on a draw. Jake decleated his man at right guard and Elle Davis got a good block on his man. But the linebackers were up on the line of scrimmage and one of them got free to make the tackle.

First down. Cobb exploded on *47 sweep* for 10 yards, running over tacklers to the Saguaro 49 yard line.

First down. Davey off right tackle on *34 belly* for three yards.

Second down. Davey ran *32 trap* up the middle, but the Saguaro safety, who was lined up only 5 yards off the line of scrimmage, made the tackle after a three yard gain.

Third down. Davey again, this time on *33 belly* behind Clay and Goody. Not quite enough for a first down–just 3 yards.

Fourth down, the ninth play of this drive. Coach Estabrook decided to go with the play that had worked so well on this drive–*47 sweep* with Cobb. Griffin went to influence block the defensive end, but got tied up with him. Therefore, Mike Reisner, who was pulling from his guard position, ran by him. The Saguaro defensive end slipped through and tackled Cobb just short of the first down.

The Saguaro defense had held. It was a good sign for Walt Sword. They needed to stop Chaparral's powerful offensive machine on this first drive. Now he needed his offense to get a long, time-consuming drive off.

On the first play, Brigham took the handoff from his quarterback, Ryan Dobson, and ran off tackle to his left, but Matt Kelley had broken through the line, and hit him behind the line of scrimmage. The ball popped out; Matt Way fell on it, but the referee ruled that his knee had hit the ground before the fumble.

Second down. This time it was Brigham over right tackle for a gain of one yard.

On third down, a pitch to Andrew Turner, the Saguaro tailback, who was swamped by a host of Chaparral tacklers for no gain.

The Firebirds were excited, and they lined up on fourth down expecting to block the punt. The rush on the attempted block was a hard one, and they almost got it. The punter quickly punched the ball to keep it from getting blocked. It travelled from the Saguaro 25 to the Chaparral 43, a 32 yard punt.

Chaparral had great field position.

On first down, Griffin ran *26 power* to his right, found the hole clogged up, reversed field to his left and ran down the left sidelines to the Saguaro 41, where he lowered his shoulder and leveled the Saguaro safety. Griffin had always been a quick, elusive runner, but now his running style was getting to be more physical when he was about to be tackled. Coach Scott Heideman's work with Griffin and Cobb had started to pay off.

First down after the 16 yard gain. Coach Estabrook was hoping to trap the aggressive Sabercat defensive tackles and called *31 trap,* but it only gained two yards.

Second down. Griffin ran *24 counter* for four yards.

Third down. Cobb ran *45 power* for two yards. Saguaro's defense had stiffened. They were gaining confidence on each play.

Fourth down. A big play for Chaparral. They did not want to get stopped again on fourth down. The Firebirds needed two yards.

Scott faked to Davey on *33 belly* and then handed off to Griffin on *24 counter*. He lost two yards.

The Saguaro defense was jumping up and down excitedly as they ran off the field. They looked like they were atop pogo sticks. And they had good reason to gloat–they had just stuffed Chaparral for the second time on fourth down.

The Firebird's knew they were in trouble. They obviously had begun to question themselves. Usually on a tough fourth down play, Coach Estabrook would call Jerry Schwartzberg's number, and he usually produced with his big, hard, tough running style, breaking tackles in his wake. They didn't have that option now. Surely, those thoughts went through Jerry's mind as he sat on the bench, his crutches beside him.

Saguaro took over on their own 34 yard line with renewed confidence. In 12 plays they would score the game's first touchdown.

The big play for the Cats was a 22 yard pass play on a botched coverage by Chaparral, from the Chaparral 35 to the 13.

With first down on the 13, Brigham had lost seven yards.

From the 20, Dobson made a great play on second down as he rolled to his left. Just as Matt Way was about to tackle him, Dobson literally pushed the ball to Turner, who ran it to the six yard line.

Coach Sword apparently had decided that it was now time to run his unbalanced line with the tight end split out five yards, and the wide receiver lined up in the slot, one yard deep, between the tight end and the tackle. (See Appendix II) Saguaro now outnumbered Chaparral, as Chaparral's line and linebackers didn't make the adjustment by shifting over one man with the unbalanced line.

Unbalanced left. Brigham took a pitch from Dobson and ran wide to his left for four yards to the two yard line.

This time, the Cats lined up unbalanced right. Brigham off tackle to his right for no gain.

Third down. Big down for both teams. Unbalanced right again. Dobson rolled out to his right and threw the ball into the end zone to his wide receiver, Conrad Loney. But Camello got his hand on the ball and deflected it off Loney's helmet. Before it could drop to the ground harmlessly, and force a Saguaro field goal on fourth down, Andrew Turner grabbed the floating ball for a touchdown.

The Saguaro stands and sidelines went crazy as the players on the field mobbed Turner. The snap on the extra point bounced on the ground; the holder picked it up and threw a desperation pass which fell incomplete in the end zone. 6-0.

Saguaro had the momentum now and it would only get better for them. Rubino, kicking off into the wind, punched the ball towards Cobb standing on the 10 yard line. Cobb picked up the bouncing ball, and as he was being tackled at the 17 yard line a Saguaro player stripped the ball and fell on it. It was Ryan Cobb's first and only fumble of the year.

In 48 seconds, Saguaro scored again as Dobson faked to his tailback running off right tackle and rolled right untouched for 15 yards and another touchdown.

This time on the extra point Dobson faked to his tailback again, dropped straight back and hit Brigham in the end zone for the two points. Brigham jumped between two Firebird defenders and caught the ball. 14-0.

Again, the Saguaro sidelines erupted. They were taking it to the number one ranked team (in power points) in the State.

On the next kickoff, Rubino again punched the ball toward Cobb. It was obvious that they wanted to keep the ball away from Griffin. Cobb picked the ball up off the ground, started up the middle and then cut to his right behind his blocker, running hard all the way to his 35 yard line before being tackled. It was a nice return.

Four plays later, Chaparral was forced to punt, and as Griffin (Hogue's leg hurt him to punt) leaned down to pick up David Williams' low snap, his right knee just barely touched the ground. Barely touched the ground to stop the play, and as the Chaparral stands moaned, and Saguaro's roared, Griffin's punted ball was brought back, and Saguaro took over on the Chaparral 31.

Chaparral was in retreat—a tipped pass for a TD by Saguaro, a fumble on the ensuing kickoff which led to a TD, and now an unusual play of a touched knee on the ground on an attempted punt. What else could go wrong?

Chaparral's defense knew that they had to step up. They seemed to be quietly confident as they took the field. After six plays, Chaparral had held.

Fourth down from the 17. Rubino kicked a 34 yard field goal from the left hash. 17-0.

On the next kickoff, Cobb, running hard straight up the middle, returned the Saguaro kickoff to his 40 yard line. Coach Estabrook decided to start throwing. He had noticed that the safety was lined up very close to the line of scrimmage.

On this next series though, Scott was sacked two out of the three plays, and a *28 sweep* by Griffin gained no yards. Chaparral was forced to punt again. Griffin got off a 33 yard punt to the Saguaro 37.

Saguaro went to a shotgun formation with only Dobson lined up behind the center. There were no backs blocking for him. He had three receivers on one side and two on another. Dobson completed a couple of short passes to open receivers who were tackled immediately. Not enough yardage for a first down though, and the Cats were forced to punt. Again, Chaparral put good pressure on the punter so that he quickly had to punch the ball. This time it went 19 yards.

Chaparral got off nine plays before the half. Scott was sacked three times, and Cobb caught two passes for 27 yards. Time ran out as David Williams was stopped after an eight yard gain on a draw.

In the Saguaro locker room at halftime, Walt Sword related to me after the season that he had told his coaches, "Look, Chaparral is too good a football team not to score on us. Their coaches are going to come up with something. Don't panic if they score. We need to keep our poise."

Walt felt very fortunate to be up 17-0. They had gotten three good breaks in the tipped ball for a TD, a fumble on the kickoff that set up the next TD, and the punter's knee touching the ground, which was the equivalent of another turnover. That had led to a field goal. He also was concerned about Andrew Turner being hurt. Turner not only gave him speed to the outside, from his tailback position, but he gave the team speed at his cornerback position on defense. The sophomore who took Turner's place on defense wasn't as fast and wasn't as experienced.

The Saguaro team had come into the locker room fired up and excited, and now as they were getting ready to go back out for the second half, Walt tried to get them settled down. "Great job guys. I'm proud of you. You're takin' it to 'em. Here's what's going to happen the second half. We're going to get the ball three times, and they're going to get the ball three times. We need to score at least once. We can do it. And as for their three possessions, we need to stop them just once. Okay? Let's go.."

Walt's prediction of the second half was almost prophetic. It was an unusual prediction because most teams had the ball at least five or six times a half–not three.

In the Chaparral locker room it was business as usual. This team did not ever seem to get way up emotionally or way down. These were unusually mature young men, and they were handling this present situation with concern–not emotion.

The coaches led by example as Ron Estabrook met with his offensive line and quickly went over the blocking assignments on a few running plays which he thought would work.

Their safety was lined up too close to the line of scrimmage and was favoring the strong side. He also decided not to pass out of his "trips" formation or the "ace" formation. Those formations only had one man to block for Scott–Saguaro was blitzing two linebackers when they saw those formations. Scott had been sacked five times in the first half. Ron went over a few more adjustments, and he was ready.

Dana Zupke had been worried all week about Brigham pounding the ball inside from tackle-to-tackle. And he was worried about Dobson on his rollouts, especially when he sprinted out and had Brigham blocking the outside linebacker, which gave Dobson time to throw.

Dana made a couple of adjustments at halftime with his defense. First, he put his ends in a "go" technique having them charge straight up the field, instead of coming down tight behind the line of scrimmage. That would force Brigham to block the end and leave the linebacker free to either force Dobson to throw quickly, or to tackle him.

The second adjustment that Dana made was to get the defensive line to shift over one man to the strong unbalanced side. This meant that on the side of the line which had four offensive men, the defensive linemen would treat the guard as the center. This would keep Saguaro from outflanking us and having more offensive men on that side than we had defenders. It was an important adjustment.

Also, Dana wasn't happy with the way that we were lining up against their shotgun formation. We were leaving a man uncovered when they lined up with five quick receivers, either on the line of scrimmage or one yard off of it.

He reminded the linebackers of what we had done in the Greenway game—same thing, the linebacker on the side with three receivers would take one of them man-to-man, and the linebacker on the side away from the three receivers would then blitz the quarterback.

While the teams were in their respective locker rooms, an unusual scene was unfolding outside. The Chaparral students, hundreds of them, did a stupid thing. They ran across the field and standing in front of the Saguaro stands, began to chant, "Saguaro sucks, Saguaro sucks!"

In response, the Saguaro fans pointed fingers toward the scoreboard and chanted, "Scoreboard! Scoreboard!"

John Kriekard, the Chaparral principal, was obviously embarrassed by his student body's demonstration and quickly moved across the field to disperse the crowd before the ugly scene got more serious. Both teams were unaware of what was happening. It would have been something of which our players and coaches would not have been proud. To taunt another team's fans was very wrong and to do that when you are getting beaten is grossly stupid.

As the teams came onto the field for the second half, Jerry Schwartzberg, on his crutches, went up to Darren Urban, The Tribune sportswriter, who was standing on our sideline behind our bench. "Darren," he said, "we're going to win this game." He waved one crutch as though to punctuate his prediction. A rather startled Darren just smiled at the gutsy statement which seemed a little too optimistic in light of the first half.

The second half began and Griffin, with the wind behind him, kicked the ball into the end zone. Saguaro started on their own 20. Saguaro had lined up five men on the 50 yard line, and four more five yards right behind those, as this formation suggested they were expecting an onside kick.

This first possession was a big one for both teams. If Saguaro could get a long drive going and score, it was going to be almost impossible for Chaparral to come back and win. But if Chaparral could stop the Cats, it would shift the momentum of the game. The Firebirds definitely needed a change in the momentum after their disastrous first half.

The fans on both sides of the field, the players and coaches seemed to anticipate that this was going to be the most exciting half of a football game they had either ever seen or played in.

The Chaparral defense was determined to stop the Cats and give the ball to their offense. We needed touchdowns, quickly!

First down. Brigham ran over his right tackle for no gain as Ryan Sydnor, the left end, knifed in to make the tackle.

Second down. Dobson faked the ball to his tailback and rolled out to his right on a quarterback keeper. But before he could break it, Matt Willden came up from his safety position and tackled him for a five yard gain.

Third and five. Dobson sprinted out to his left, stopped and threw a pass to his receiver running a five yard "out" pattern. Larry Zak, our right cornerback, played it perfectly. He stepped in front of the receiver, looked up at the wide open 30 yards in front of him for a TD....and dropped the ball. He didn't look the ball into his hands. The Chaparral crowd groaned. This could have been the momentum changer. No one felt worse about it than Larry. A couple of his teammates tried to console him.

Fourth down. We had come close to blocking a couple of punts. If we could block a punt that would turn the energy toward our favor. We had preached and preached to our kids the importance of special teams and how they could change the momentum of games.

145

Again, as the punter caught the ball from his snapper, he was rushed hard. Larry Zak and Austin Sendlein just missed blocking the punt. The punter, in his hurry to get the ball off to keep it from being blocked, got off a 17 yard punt.

We were in business on the Saguaro 42 yard line–great field position.

On the first play, Ron called *31 dive*–no trap blocking, just one-on-one blocking behind Mike Reisner at left guard.

Before David Willliams even got to the line of scrimmage, our center, Don Kaufman, had turned his man to the right. Mike went after the linebacker and turned him to his right. Adam Goodworth hit the defensive tackle lined up over him, and turned him to his left. Clay had no one lined up over him, so he started running straight downfield looking for the safety. All Davey saw after Scott handed him the ball was a big open hole. He took off for the end zone, first passing Clay, as he ran, and then running past the safety. Touchdown!

The Chaparral sidelines and stands exploded. The band began to play the fight song as Ryan Cobb kicked the extra point straight through the middle of the uprights. 17-7, Saguaro. There was 10:18 left in the third quarter.

Saguaro returned Griffin's kickoff to their 30, where they started their next possession.

On third down, we thought that we had them stopped, but our middle linebacker, Austin Sendlein, was flagged for an interference penalty on a short pass over the middle.

First down on their 45. Brigham then ran the ball four straight times for a total of 23 yards.

Saguaro went into their unbalanced slot formation for five straight plays, again running Brigham on four of them for 13 yards.

On the fifth play, Dobson faked to Brigham, and threw incomplete to Jon Rentschler on the 10 yard line. After the ball went over his head, Willden, in his over-zealousness, hit Rentzler and the flag was thrown–unnecessary roughness–15 yard penalty to the 10 yard line.

First down. Brigham ran a sweep to his right for five yards.

Second down. Brigham again ran a sweep to the right, cut it up and was tackled at the 3 yard line.

Chaparral had to hold. A touchdown by the Sabercats would put the game out of reach. They were eating time off the clock. This drive had started with 10:18 to go in the third quarter. Now with only 2:15 to go, this drive had eaten up eight minutes.

Third down. Dobson rolled out to his right and cut it up before he was tackled on the one. But wait a minute...there was a flag on the ground...

The Saguaro tailback had moved just before the ball was snapped. The five yard penalty moved the ball back to the eight yard line. Instead of having fourth down on the one yard line, it was third down on the eight.

Dobson took a three step drop and threw a quick out to Rentschler on the goal line. Larry Zak hit him, just as Rentschler got his hands on the ball, and knocked the ball to the ground. Important play. Big play.

Fourth down. In came Rubino for the field goal. He kicked it from the left hash mark–a 25 yard field goal. 20-7, Saguaro.

There was still plenty of time, even though Saguaro had run off 16 plays in eight minutes. The Chaparral sidelines seemed to read my thoughts, "Still plenty of time," they chanted.

Rubino again kicked off to Cobb who returned it from the 15 to our 32 yard line.

First down. *32 trap* by Davey. One yard gain.

Second down. Ron wanted to run left behind Clay and Mike again, and attack Saguaro's right side–*wing right,* get the safety over to that side. *33 belly.* Clay turned out on his man, Mike blocked the linebacker and Griffin led the way through the hole, making a key block, as Davey, running right in front of the Chaparral bench, sprinted 19 yards to the Saguaro 48. This sudden shift in momentum seemed to infuse the players and stands with new life.

First down. *32 trap* for two yards.

Second down. Cobb made a nice run of six yards on *47 sweep,* but we were caught holding. The ball went back to our 49 on the penalty.

Second down, again. Scott faked *34 belly* to Davey, dropped back and threw a perfect pass down the right sideline to Cobb, who was behind the Saguaro defensive back. He was immediately tackled on the 18. It was an important play on Chaparral's behalf by both Scott and Ryan Cobb.

First down. *33 belly* gained only three yards.

It was now the fourth quarter. Ron decided to run *33 belly* again on second down.

He felt confident in running behind Clay and Mike. This time, Davey ran for six yards to the eight yard line.

Third and one. Ron called *32 trap*. Tonight, *32 trap* wasn't working. No gain.

Fourth and one. Saguaro called a time out. Scott took the snap from Kaufmann and followed him, making the one yard easily.

First down. Behind Clay and Mike again, *33 belly* for four yards as little Josh Griffin got a great block on Brigham.

Second down on the three yard line. Scott pivots to his left and fakes the ball to Davey on *33 belly*. Saguaro is expecting it, as the linebackers and defensive backs react to Davey. After Scott's fake, he hands the ball to Griffin on *24 counter*. Griffin runs behind Clay's block to his right and cuts up the field for the necessary three yards and a touchdown.

Pandemonium in the Chaparral stands reached a fevered pitch. It wouldn't have surprised me to see the stadium lights shatter.

Cobb's kick was good. It was now 20-14, Saguaro, with 10:39 to go in the fourth quarter. Still plenty of time.

Saguaro again lined up nine men close to the 50 yard line, expecting an onside kick. Griffin pooched it left to the 25 yard line, and Davey Williams almost recovered it before a Saguaro player fell on it.

After a first down by Saguaro, Chaparral held and forced the Saguaro punter, under pressure again, to punt the ball out of bounds. In addition, a Saguaro player was called on a face mask penalty for 15 yards.

We started the next drive, only the third one of the half, and as I later found out, just what Walt Sword had predicted, on our own 46. Great field position after the short punt and penalty.

Third down. Scott faked the ball to Davey again on *33 belly*, and dropped back to pass. He threw the ball to Griffin, but it was incomplete. Suddenly the Chaparral bench exploded as a flag was thrown–interference on Saguaro. The penalties which had gone against Chaparral earlier were now evening out.

First down on the 41 of Saguaro. Scott faked *33 belly* to Davey again, and gave the ball to Griffin on *24 counter.* Griffin broke a tackle and made just three yards. After a five yard offside penalty against Saguaro, the ball was on the 33.

Second down. *33 belly* for one yard. Someone up front missed a block.

Third down. Big down. Chaparral needed a big play. Scott pitched the ball to Griffin running to his left on *27 pitch.* A Saguaro defender broke through and seemed to have Griffin tackled, but he broke it and then ran over the defensive back for a one yard gain and a first down.

First down on the 28. Again, *33 belly* as Ron continued to attack Saguaro's right side behind Clay and Mike. Davey ran for eight yards and Griffin made a great lead block. The little guy was developing into quite a blocker.

Second and two. Ron crossed up the defense by calling a hitch pattern to our wide receiver, John Hogue. Complete. He was tackled immediately. Six yard gain.

First down. The ball was on the 14, and Ron called "old reliable"–*33 belly* again. Behind Goody, Clay and Griffin, Davey hit the hole and began weaving his way to the one yard line for a 13 yard gain.

First down from the one yard line. The Chaparral fans were on their feet in anticipation of the touchdown, screaming at a volume which threatened to cover Scott's voice barking out his signals, "Shift, set go," and the ball was snapped.

Scott pivoted to his left and ran the "play of the day" handing off to Davey on *33 belly*. Davey cut back to his right as the hole closed up, and scored standing up. 20-20!

The crowd became unusually quiet. A strange hush blanketed the stadium when Chaparral lined up for the extra point. The next moment could change everything for either team. This kick was poised on the threshold of a championship.

Perfect snap from David Williams, "the jack of all trades," a perfect hold by Matt Willden, and a superb kick by Ryan Cobb. "Pressure? What pressure?" Ryan told us a few seconds later on the sidelines. 21-20, Chaparral.

We dared not take a deep breath–this game was not over yet–not by a long shot. There was still 4:05 left and a very dangerous tandem of Brigham running and Dobson passing.

Griffin, again pooched the kickoff to the left, on Saguaro's 32, where they fell on it. We didn't want to kick it deep and give their returner a chance to break one. Also, we were kicking against the wind.

On first down, Dobson hit his wide receiver on the right, running on a short out for three yards. But Camello missed the tackle, and Willden finally pushed him out of bounds on the 50.

First down again. This time, they ran the same play, but Chris Medill, who had taken Camello's place, came up and made a hard tackle on the receiver, holding him to a three yard gain.

Second down. Saguaro ran the same play for the third straight time, and Medill again nailed him for a one yard gain. But there was a motion penalty.

Second down over again. Dobson rolled out to his left and was under pressure from Matt Kelley, who was executing his "go" technique that Dana Zupke had instituted at halftime. Dobson threw the ball–incomplete.

On third down, from the Saguaro 39, Dobson faked to Brigham running over right tackle and dropped back to pass. Under pressure, he got the ball off to Brigham over the middle for a 15 yard gain to our 36 yard line. This great play kept their drive alive.

Now the Saguaro stands and sidelines fervently urged their team on. Our sidelines seemed to be biting their nails. We had worked too hard to overcome that 17-0 deficit to throw it away by letting them score. A verbal duel ensued as Firebirds fans shouted "defense, defense!"

First down on our 32. Dobson faked the ball to his tailback, running over right tackle, and then dropped back and hit his receiver, Eric Salnas, on a 21 yard pass down the middle to our 15 yard line. The pass had been thrown just over Bies' outstretched arms.

On first down, Dobson handed the ball off to Brigham over right tackle. Two yard gain.

It was now obvious to the Chaparral coaches that Saguaro was not going to call timeouts' to stop the clock, or throw passes which might stop the clock, or take a chance on an interception. Their very obvious strategy was to run the clock down to keep us from having any time left after they kicked a field goal.

I grabbed Ryan Cobb on the sidelines. "I want you to take Zack Bies' place on the field goal block team. You're quicker off the ball than he is."

Ryan nodded.

"I want you to come tight off the wing's outside shoulder, so that he blocks you. That will open up a gap for Jake to get through."

It was now second down, and this time they ran Brigham over left guard for 3 yards. The clock was ticking down. We were running out of time.

Next I grabbed Davey Williams on the sidelines, "Davey, I'm going to change something. Listen up...you take Matt Way's place on the field goal block team." Usually the right linebacker on the field goal block team lines up in front of the end, but does not rush to block the kick. His job is to take the end, man-to-man, if it is a faked field goal.

Davey's eyes were wide, trying to grasp the new strategy. "I want you to forget about covering the end. I want you to line up on his inside shoulder and go for the block. If he blocks you, Jake should get through. If he doesn't block you...it's yours."

Davey nodded and smiled. I wasn't worried about his executing something which we had not practiced. He was a very savvy football player. It was desperation time, and we needed to do desperate things. If Saguaro faked a field goal and threw to their left end, I was going to be in deep trouble. But it was a risk I was willing to take.

Third down. Saguaro lined up in their unbalanced slot right formation. Jake, from his middle linebacker position, knew what they were going to run. Earlier, when they had lined up in that same formation, they had run sweep right. As Dobson pivoted to his right and pitched the ball to Brigham, Jake broke through the guard and tackle hole, catching Brigham from behind for a four yard loss. Big play by Jake!

The ball was on the 14 yard line and the right hash mark as Mike Rubino trotted out to kick the game winning field goal.

There were 43 seconds left and Ron called time out. If they made the field goal, he wanted at least a shot at moving the ball close enough for our own field goal attempt.

On the sidelines, Jerry, with his crutches in one hand, said, "We're going to win this, Mr. Urban."

I jogged out onto the field favoring my artificial hip. Gathering the block team around, I reviewed each person's responsibility. As I loped back to the sidelines the thought presented itself that we had an excellent chance of blocking it, but the pounding of my heart and mouth full of cotton seemed to be telling me exactly the opposite. I couldn't seem to swallow.

The ball was snapped to the holder and just as Rubino approached the ball, three white-shirted figures penetrated the black jersey line of blockers. Cobb had done exactly as I had expected him to do. His quickness off the ball forced the wing to step out and block him. That left a hole for Jake. He just needed to get there in time. For some reason, the end did not block down on Davey, maybe it was because this was the first time all night he had rushed from that linebacker spot.

Both Jake and Davey arrived at the kicked ball just as it left Rubino's foot. Both got their hand on the ball.

The noise was that wonderful "splat" sound—music to the defensive team's ears.

The ball bounced to our left where Camello tried to grab it, but before he could get his arms around, Mike Reisner fell on it.

The Chaparral stands went berzerk.

Jerry turned again to Darren Urban, "See, I told you that we could do it. I knew we were going to win!"

Scott took a knee and let the clock run out the final few seconds. The Chaparral stands started emptying as the students began flooding onto the field. It was like a dam break.

As I turned around and watched this huge mob of people coming at me, fear suddenly hit. I was in the path of this pulsing, crushing stampede. My moment of cowardice stemmed from having an artificial hip, and I was afraid I wouldn't be able to dodge this sudden, screaming avalanche of people.

And they did come straight at me as they pounded onto the field, mobbing the Chaparral team. I stood frozen, not moving, and to my great relief, the students melted around me like I was a post driven into the ground.

While the mob scene in the middle of the field was going on, I turned and walked across the field to shake Walt Sword's hand. His first words were, "You know, I think that this was the best football game I have ever seen."

"I totally agree with you," I told him. "I don't think I've ever been this excited before in my life about a football game."

After a few more words, I moved back to the middle of the field where I shook hands with the Saguaro players as they were headed to the south end zone to meet with their coaches.

They were great warriors. They had played a very courageous game and as I shook each player's hand, each one responded in a gracious manner, especially Ryan Dobson.

"Good luck, Coach," he told me, "I hope you go all the way."

Walt Sword could be proud of his young men. He had brought respectability back to a program which had lost respect under a different coach, two years ago. This team practiced sportsmanship and even though they had lost the game, they had gone out winners in a sense.

Jerry tried to dance on his crutches. "See, I told you we'd do it for you, man." Jake exclaimed.

The atmosphere on the bus ride back to Chaparral resembled the hilarity of a party. However, if someone had stood up and announced that they would be behind Tempe 14-7 in the second quarter this time next week, there might have been a slight hush, but most likely that statement would have been met with derisive laughter. They felt that they were invincible.

The scenario was clear however: if we didn't beat Tempe next week, and we lost the Conference championship, this game with Saguaro would mean nothing. It was a sobering thought spelled out to the players by Coach Estabrook the next morning, when their colorful victory balloon settled gently back down to earth.

CHAPTER ELEVEN

"TEMPE–FOR THE CONFERENCE CHAMPIONSHIP"

In the game against Saguaro we did have the usual statistical dominance. In fact, the Firebirds had gone four straight quarters without scoring a touchdown–the last two quarters in the Apache Junction game, and the first two quarters in the Saguaro game.

We had rushed for 227 yards against the Cats, and thrown for 81 yards on four out of six attempts for a total of 296 yards. This was almost 100 yards below our average per game.

David Williams had run for 131 yards in 18 carries at fullback, averaging 7.3 yards per carry and scoring two TD's.

Josh Griffin had run for 52 yards on eight carries for a 6.5 average and one touchdown. He had also caught a pass for 13 yards.

Ryan Cobb had another good all round game, gaining 44 yards on seven carries for a 6.3 average, catching two passes for 62 yards, and returning three kickoffs for 59 yards.

Dana Zupke was extremely happy with his defense, especially in the second half. They had held Saguaro to only 114 yards rushing on 39 carries, for less than three yards per carry. We were the first team to hold Brigham to less than three yards per carry. Dobson had a good game, completing 11 for 16 for 113 yards, but

Chaparral stopped his passing in the second half. Their total offense rushing and passing was 229 yards.

The defensive leaders for the Firebirds were: Zach Bies with 18 tackle points; Chris Dobbins with 12; Larry Zak, Matt Willden and Jake Ireland with 11; and Austin Sedlein and Matt Kelley had 10 each.

Saguaro was behind us now. In front of our now rolling train on the Championship track was Tempe High School, who seemed to have a split personality. They had been State Champions the year before, and earlier in the season had knocked off the number one team in the State at that time. But then they had been upset by Saguaro and Coronado in the past two weeks. They were dangerous. They had a huge line, and fast running backs, especially their little tailback, R.J. Norwood, who, when it came to quickness and speed, was in Griffin's class.

We also had a lot of respect for Tim McBurney, the Tempe coach. He had led them to a State championship the year before and his teams were always fundamentally sound. We put him in the same league with Joe Corte.

That Friday night in late October there was a crisp chill in the air. Tempe kicked off to us. In three plays after taking over on our 27, Griffin, from the Tempe 45 yard line, had followed David Williams on *26 power.* Then, behind blocks downfield by Clay and Jake, who decleated their men, he had sprinted by the last defenders for a touchdown. 7-0.

On our kickoff to Tempe after the touchdown, I made a mistake. I told Griffin to pooch the ball instead of kicking it deep. They had changed their alignment in the film which we had seen, and they had their end on that side in perfect position. He caught it at his 31 and returned it to the 45 yard line. My poor decision made for a short field.

At mid-field, with fourth and a couple of yards to go, Tempe ran a fake punt for a first down. They scored on that first drive in 13 plays, which took just over five minutes. 7-7.

On their kickoff to us, they also tried a pooch. Medill caught it on our 40, returned it to the 49, and then another 15 yards was tacked on because of a Tempe face mask penalty. After seven plays, we had a fourth down on their 32, but on *47 waggle* Scott threw an incompletion.

On Tempe's first play, the Tempe fullback, Philip Cassals, ran to his right, off tackle. Mike Reisner over-ran him, and as he cut back to the middle of the field, Matt Way over-ran him. He sprinted by our defensive backs for a 68 yard TD run. 14-7 Tempe.

After the kickoff on our next series, David Williams fumbled on the 50 yard line and Tempe recovered.

Concern blanketed our sidelines. Here we were, down 14-7 and had given them the ball on our 46. The momentum was building on the Tempe side of the ball.

Then on second down, Brad Reisner, our right defensive tackle, broke through the line, grabbed the ball carrier on a counter play, as he was getting the ball from the quarterback. He stripped the ball from him and fell on it. Our sidelines exploded.

On first down, Griffin broke loose on *26 power* again, but as he was being tackled, he fumbled the ball and Tempe recovered. In four successive plays there had been three fumbles.

It was an emotional yo-yo for both teams. We hadn't fumbled twice in a game all year. And now, in two successive offensive plays we had butter-fingers.

Our defense held them on four plays and after the punt, we took over on our 25.

In eight plays we scored, with one long run from Davey on *33 belly* for 31 yards. And then Griffin ran for 13 yards to the 11 yard line. Cobb scored on *47 sweep* with a good block by Hogue on their cornerback. 14-14.

After holding Tempe again for four downs, it took 10 plays in three minutes for Davey to score on *33 belly* behind Jake, Ellie Davis, our right tackle, and Goodworth and Cobb's blocks. Davey scored standing up from the eight yard line. 21-14.

The first half had been an emotional roller coaster for the coaching staff. I was walking off the field at halftime and ran into my wife, Linda, and a good friend, Tim Gay. I told them, "I'm getting too old for this. I don't think that my heart is going to take much more of this."

Chaparral kicked off to start the second half. The first defensive series of the half is always a big one. On this series, Zach Bies came up with another big play, intercepting a pass on the Tempe 35.

Tempe's defense stiffened and it took five minutes and 10 tough plays before Scott hit John Hogue on a five yard slant for a TD. 27-14.

Again our defense stopped the Tempe offense on their next possession. We took over after their punt to us on our 38.

On first down, Davey popped *32 trap* for 57 yards to the Tempe five, but we had an illegal motion penalty which brought the ball back to our 33.

It took 13 plays on the drive, which was helped by a roughing-the-punter penalty against Tempe. We finally scored when Scott hit Griffin in the end zone on a wheel pattern for nine yards. Griffin made a nice catch as he out-jumped the taller Tempe defender. 33-14.

Tempe scored another touchdown late in the fourth quarter on a halfback pass for 73 yards. Final score, 33-20.

In the last six minutes we had another long drive that ended on the Tempe three, when Ron instructed Scott to drop to his knee, running the clock out which kept us from scoring. Ron had a lot of respect for Tim McBurney and there was no need to score another touchdown with a minute to go. Ron's approach to other coaches was one of respect. He felt that we were "all in the same fraternity" as he liked to say. Our philosophy was to respect our opponents, their players and coaches, and to never criticize or gossip about the problems which another coach might have. It could be "us" in those shoes; therefore, he instructed Scott not to run up the score further.

We had clinched the East Sky Region championship, even though we had one game to go against Arcadia.

It was the first step on our way to ASU and the Sun Devil Stadium, to play in the State Championship game.

The coaches and players both knew that Davey could play, and he proved it this night, running for 211 yards in 27 carries for a 7.8 yard average and a TD.

Griffin again had a very productive night, running the ball 13 times for 123 yards and a 9.5 average. He also caught two passes for 24 yards and 2 TD's.

Ryan Cobb rushed for 82 yards on 14 carries for a 5.9 yard average, and one TD.

The three of them had rushed for 407 yards against a good Tempe defense. Scott was 7 for 17 and 72 yards, plus 2 TD's, which gave the offense a total of 489 yards.

The defense had stepped up again. If you took out the long 68 yard run by Cassals, Tempe only had 71 yards rushing on 30 attempts for a 2.3 yard average. Our front seven had definitely outplayed their bigger offensive line. They completed 5 for 12, passing for 92 yards, but 73 of that came on the halfback pass late in the game.

Our sophomore linebacker, Austin Sendlein was improving in broad strides each game, as he led the team in tackle points with 13.

Jake Ireland and Matt Way both had 10, and Mike Reisner eight.

Next was Arcadia. It was a team that we should beat. They were playing a lot of sophomores and their quarterback, Matt Cooley, had sustained a season ending injury just two weeks before.

We needed to win this one to go 10 and 0. Could we keep up the intensity and not let up against a team that we should beat?

THE TURNAROUND

CHAPTER TWELVE

"ARCADIA - 10 AND 0"

The Tempe game had been Adam Goodworth's best game. He was in the "zone" the entire game. Clay Muschinski, who was improving with each game, had a number of decleaters in the Tempe game. On one play he had knocked his man to the ground, falling with him, and while on the ground he saw the little Tempe safety running by him. Clay sprang from the ground and decleated him also, getting two decleaters on one play. He had had trouble with their All-State linebacker, Josh McBurney, who would slip the block by Clay and make the tackle after a four or five yard gain. Clay adjusted his technique from blocking him high to blocking him low at the waist, and he was able to hold his block longer on McBurney. This enabled Davey Williams to break some long runs in the second half.

Matt Way knew that Tempe would be tough. Their line was big, as usual, but the second half of the Saguaro game had proven to him that this team had overcome the absence of Jerry. He felt that Jerry's injury had forced the team to play more cohesively— the team had become closer, in order to make up for the loss of Jerry.

Jake Ireland told me he felt the Tempe game had been his best offensive game of the year. He was banged up from the

161

Saguaro game and his sprained ankle was bothering him, but he felt that it served to make him focus more. Also, he didn't have to play defense. Austin Sendlein was doing a good job, and it gave him time to rest his ankle.

Jerry watched this game from the sideline. He had thrown away his crutches and now had a large brace on his right knee, which made him limp when he walked. His rehab was going even better than expected and he was going to do some light running the following week. The week after that he hoped to be ready to play in the first playoff game.

Coach Zupke had made a key defensive adjustment at half-time against Tempe. They had shown a new formation, with their backs lined up in a strong formation to the wingback side. It gave them an extra blocker there. Dana adjusted his linebacker and brought one of his safeties up to the line. The defense shut Tempe down in the second half.

This week Dana Zupke was concerned about Arcadia's passing game and their big offensive line.

It was a cool November night. Arcadia kicked off. Josh Griffin got us off to a good start when he returned the opening kickoff 95 yards for a touchdown, behind great blocks by Mike Reisner and Zach Bies. And then Arcadia went on a long drive inside our ten yard line, where we put on a goal line stand. They had run the ball straight at us and we were having trouble with the size of their linemen, who were dominating us at the line of scrimmage. But after we held them, the game turned into a rout.

We took over on our 10 yard line, Scott hit Goodworth on a pass from our 28 yard line that covered 72 yards. It was by far the longest TD catch in Goody's career, and it brought a big smile to his face as he trotted back to the sidelines after the TD. He was very well-liked by his teammates and they let him know how excited they were for him. 14-0.

Davey Williams broke off a 55 yard TD run on the next series for 20-0 lead.

John Hogue caught an 18 yard pass from Scott for a TD. Zach Bies returned an interception for 48 yards, and Davey finished the first half scoring with a 22 yard run. 40-0.

Ryan Cobb scored a 28 yard run in the third quarter and then Griffin returned a punt 68 yards for a TD. He brought a little excitement to the play, when after about ten yards, he unintentionally fumbled the ball on the ground and it bounced right back into his hands. He never missed a stride and kept on running into the end zone.

For most of the second half, the second string and junior varsity players got the playing time. Josh Utterback gained 43 yards in eight carries and one TD. Sean Holland, up from the JV squad, carried eight times for 27 yards and a TD. Ryan Benscoter, the JV quarterback, was one for one on a 12 yard pass to Mark Rittman. Final score 67-6.

Scott was 3 for 5, and 118 yards passing with 2 TD's. Our rushing offense gained a total of 297 yards, with Davey having an 18 yard average per carry on 6 carries for 108 yards and 2 TD's. Cobb had a 12 yard average on 6 carries for 72 yards and one TD. Griffin had 42 yards on five carries for an 8.4 average, and one reception pass for 28 yards, plus 2 TD's. In spite of the 109 yards in penalties, the offense had a total of 427 yards.

The defense was unbelievable, holding Arcadia to just 51 yards rushing on 34 attempts for a 1.5 yard average, and the pass defense held Arcadia to 10 of 24 for 86 yards. It was really not a fair test for Arcadia without their All-City QB, Matt Cooley. Coach Ron Vick had two outstanding wide receivers and Arcadia had been very competitive in a couple of games, especially Tempe, before Cooley had gotten injured. Cooley had thrown for almost 2,000 yards and 17 TD's in eight games before his injury.

Going into this game, the Chaparral coaching staff knew that Arcadia, without Cooley, should be a game that we would play a lot of young players. That week we had brought ten sophomores and a freshman quarterback from the junior varsity up to the varsity. Their season had ended a week before and they had another successful season under their head coach, Jim Ellison. They had lost only one game, to Greenway, and had dominated their opponents in most of their games.

Jim Ellison, a Coronado graduate, had coached Pop Warner teams in Scottsdale for many years. After a slow start in his first year, when his team started 0-4, he had compiled a record of 17 wins and 3 losses.

The varsity coaching staff was anxious to see how the "J" players, as we called them, would do against Arcadia's mostly sophomore and junior team. Arcadia seemed to be the up and coming team of the future in our Conference. How would our newest warriors, our sophomores and juniors, stack up against theirs?

Chaparral fans and supporters were familiar with sophomore Josh Griffin, who set a couple of school records and made second team All-Conference and All-City; Austin Sendlein, (whose father played in the NFL and was an All-American at the University of Texas) made All-City first team linebacker; and Brad Reisner, who made All-Conference defensive tackle.

Now the Chaparral faithful were getting a look at the players who would be replacing the 17 seniors who had done such an admirable job in leading the way, to turn the football program around. The sophomores that played against Arcadia whose names would soon be household names in Scottsdale, were Scott Lane, who started at Camello's place at cornerback when he was injured; Mike Connor, offensive guard and defensive end; John Robey, defensive tackle; Nick Iarrobino, linebacker; T.J. Geninatti, linebacker; Ryan Wilson, safety; and freshman, Alex Lazar, tackle; freshman Ryan Benscoter, quarterback; Sean Holland, running back and cornerback; and there were others, such as freshman Dustin Ireland (Jake's little brother); Cooper Bradshaw, Brad Pepe and Mark Johnson, who would be joining the varsity next season.

These young men would be joining the small junior class to make up the 1998 team. Juniors such as first team All-Conference, All-City safety Zach Bies; first team All-City linebacker and offensive guard, Mike Reisner; linemen, Dan Kaufman, Ellie Davis and Palani Luger; defensive backs, Michael Camello, John Hogue, Josh Utterback, and running back Chris Medill.

As coaches and fans watched the second half of the Arcadia game, we saw next year's team outscore Arcadia 27-6. After the game we were feeling a little bit better about the 1998 season. The coffers were being refilled.

The question was what JV coffers would Coach Ellison have to look forward to? He would be receiving, with wide open arms, an undefeated freshman team that was coached by Nick Demember. The class was the best looking group of young athletes that I had seen at Chaparral. It was no accident that 26 of them had started in our weight program the previous summer.

Our coaching staff became completely sold on this off-season program, believing that our success in 1997 was directly related to the summer work that our young men invested in. We also had 26 kids, who were going to be incoming freshmen, participate in this weight program. It was no accident that the freshmen team went 8 - 0 for this season.

The Firebird defense was led that night against Arcadia by Brad Reisner, our outstanding sophomore defensive tackle, who was just relentless. "He just keeps coming," Coach Reinhardt had said. Brad would get knocked down and then get up and be in on the tackle. He had 15 tackle points. His brother, Mike, had 15 points, Austin Sendlein had 11, and Matt Willden had 10 points.

After the game that Friday night, we met at Ruby Tuesday's, a restaurant on Shea Boulevard, about a mile from the high school. They had supported our 64 page football program with advertisements and had donated money for weights in our weight room. In turn, the Chaparral football family, which included parents, fans, players and students, would pack the restaurant after each game. It was a restaurant which featured many TV's strategically placed throughout the rooms. We would all watch "Friday Night Fever" on Channel 12, which gave the high school football scores and video shots of selected games. It was a fun experience, especially when you are winning. After the "Friday Night Fever" show, Ron Estabrook would insert a copy of the game played that night into the tape machine. We would all get to see the game played again.

By watching the "Friday Night Fever" show, we found out who would be our first playoff game opponent. We expected it to be either Flagstaff or Peoria. Chaparral had been number one all year in power points because of its tough schedule. Each team received 50 points for a win, 0 for a loss, and five points for every win that their opponent picked up over the course of the season.

We were in for a huge surprise. We waited expectantly for the scores to see who the 16th ranked team in power points would be. When it was announced, we were all in a state of disbelief. Flagstaff and Peoria had both been upset. The 16th team in the playoffs was Saguaro!

CHAPTER THIRTEEN

"SAGUARO PLAY OFF–NO MERCY"

Walt Sword was happy to be in the Playoffs. He was excited for his kids. It was a great reward for them after they had turned their season around and won their last five out of six. But he would rather have played someone other than Chaparral. As he told George Allen, the well-known Cox Cable broadcaster, who was going to televise the game on a tape-delayed basis, "We're either going to have a close game like before, or Chaparral is going to blow us away."

The Chaparral coaches had mixed feelings. Coach Estabrook didn't like to play a team in the Playoffs which he had already beaten. A couple of the Chaparral assistants were really anxious to play Saguaro again. I was included in that category. We wanted to show them and the "football community" in the State that we were really a better football team than the one which had previously squeaked by Saguaro 21-20. We wanted to make sure our kids were focused on this game. I had my wife, Linda, make up two "No Mercy" signs with Saguaro on them.

Matt Way's statement seemed to represent a consensus of the team's attitude. "They (Saguaro players) were telling the papers that they wanted another shot at us, because they thought we got lucky when we beat them. Now is the time to get revenge on our first game against them. They wanted us...and they got us." And later, after the game, Matt said, "They got us—in fact, they got the best of us." It was a surprising statement from a quiet young man, who normally didn't have much to say.

Clay Mushinski made it known that he really didn't want to play Saguaro again, since we had already beaten them. He wanted somebody new, but made the statement, "We have to play somebody, so let's go out and beat them."

Jake was fired up. His buddy, Jerry, was going to suit up and play. Jerry had not looked quite as good as before the injury, during practice this week; however, he looked good enough.

Goody felt this was a big game for the seniors. They needed to play well. "It's going to be my best game of this season," he told all of us.

It was unusual, but four teams out of the East Sky Conference had made the 16 team 4A State Playoffs: Chaparral was seeded first with a 10 and 0 record; Tempe, with a 6-3-1 record, was seeded 10th; Coronado, with a 6 and 4 record was seeded 14th; and Saguaro with a 6-4 record was seeded 16th. It had been a good year for the East Sky Conference. No other conference had four teams in the Playoffs. It proved the point that the East Sky coaches had been making all year, that this conference was the toughest one in 4-A.

In preparation for this game, Dana Zupke kept everything simple for the defense. He had the "offensive scout team" line up in different formations and made sure that our defense was lined up correctly. "Just line up and play football," he told the defense.

Dana was not sure what Saguaro would throw at us offensively. In the first Saguaro game, the unbalanced line, with a half-back lined up in the "slot" between the tackle and the wide receiver, had surprised him. He had thanked me after the game for recognizing it immediately.

Dana is an excellent young coach who will someday become an excellent head coach. One of the most difficult skills to master as a young coach is what I call "head coach's eyes." Head coach's eyes are able to see a formation immediately when the offense lines up. Also, after a play is run, head coach's eyes can immediately pick up why a play didn't work–who missed a block–or if a back ran in the wrong hole.

Ron Estabrook had excellent 20:20 vision in that regard. In practice, when an offensive play was not run correctly, he knew immediately where the problem was. Acquiring this skill is an exercise one develops through time and experience. It was something I had managed to develop also over the years. The first thing I look for when the opposing team's offense breaks the huddle and lines up, is if it is a balanced line or unbalanced line. Having played linebacker in both high school and college, it was my responsibility to shift the defensive formation and linebackers if the opposing team lined up in a line, to try and outflank us.

Red Caughron, when he coached at Woodberry Forest (our rival prep school when I was coaching) would shift a tackle from one side to the other when his team got down near the goal line. If you didn't adjust to his having four linemen on one side of the center, it would create a big hole and there would not be enough defensive players on that side of the line.

Speaking of "coach's eyes," our position assistant coaches had very good "eyes." Scott Heideman was unusually effective at helping his running backs in their blocking, and his linebackers in reading running plays and shedding blockers. Scott is very detail oriented and his coaching of our linebackers and running backs made them better players each week.

In group work, Dana and John Reinhardt, the defensive tackle coach, worked hard with the linemen to make sure on passing plays that they stayed in their lanes and didn't leave an opening for Dobson, their quarterback, to run through.

It was a beautiful late fall night in Arizona on November 14, 1997. The stadium was packed with an overflow crowd of approximately 4,000 on both sides of the field. Saguaro had brought their band and their crowd was as rowdy as the home team, Chaparral.

Saguaro, dressed in their white jerseys, came on the field first to stretch and warm up in the pre-game ritual. Chaparral came onto the field a few minutes later, dressed in red jerseys and red pants. As the Firebirds circled the end zone and spread out over the west side of the field, Walt Sword noticed number 34, Jerry Schwartzberg's number.

He suddenly realized the rumors, which had been swirling about Jerry being able to play, were true. He glanced around at his players to see if they had seen Jerry leading the Chaparral warm ups with the three other captains. Obviously, his players had. They appeared to be distracted by Jerry's presence and stared at him while doing their own stretching exercises.

Ron and I stood beside each other, observing the reaction of the Sabercats to Jerry's appearance. Ron had initially thought Jerry might not be able to play until the next Playoff game; he wanted to watch him run, have the doctor sign off. Therefore, that was the information he gave the media; however, he told him to dress, hoping that Jerry's appearance on the field would be a distraction, and give us a psychological boost. It was like unveiling a secret weapon. We saw the Saguaro players talking to each other and nodding toward Jerry. Ron looked at me and smiled.

He now knew Jerry's doctor had just signed off, giving him permission to play. Ron's plan was to start Davey Williams and then if Jerry was needed, bring him into the game at just the moment that would charge the momentum. This would give the Firebirds a psychological lift. But his presence alone had cast an ominous cloud over the Saguaro sideline. What Ron could have had no way of knowing at that time, was that he would not need Jerry this night.

Saguaro kicked off and held the Firebirds on their first possession. After Hogue's punt, the Cats took over on their 27.

After three straight running plays by Brigham had netted only seven yards, Saguaro was forced to punt on fourth down.

Jake Ireland forced his way past the blockers, jumped in the air and hit the ball with his hand, forcing it backwards. It hit at the 12 yard line and bounced right into Larry Zak's hands. He joyfully ran into the end zone for a touchdown. The special teams were doing their "momentum thing." 7-0.

On the kickoff, Scott Lane, up from the JV team, kicked the ball high to the Saguaro 10 yard line, and the returner ran it back to his 23.

On third down, Dobson threw a quick out pattern to his inside receiver. Zach Bies read it perfectly, and he turned his fifth interception of the year into a touchdown, running it down the left sideline for 32 yards. 14-0. The Chaparral sideline and stands went crazy.

When Lane kicked off this time, the ball bounced around to the six yard line. The receiver's knee touched the ground as he tried to pick up the ball. First down for Saguaro on their 6 yard line.

The Firebird defense held and forced a punt, which Griffin almost broke loose on the return.

First down for Chaparral on the Cats 49.

Scott ran *28 waggle* and with plenty of time to throw, he found Cobb, who was "tagged," on a backside post for a 49 yard touchdown pass. The ball sailed in the air for 35 yards and it was perfect as Cobb caught the ball in stride. He ran it into the end zone. 21-0.

In a four minute time period Chaparral had scored three touchdowns, and had done it with only one offensive play.

After the touchdown and extra point, I walked out onto the field, as I usually do, to get the kicking tee from our holder, Matt Wilden. By the time I got to the huddle of our kickoff team and before I could give them my short pre-kick pep talk, I overheard Zach Bies telling them, "Don't let up...don't let 21-0 make you overconfident...no mercy...run down on this one just as hard as you did on the first kickoff–no mercy."

He saw me approaching and offered, "Sorry, Coach."

"No, Zach," I said. "That was great–couldn't have said it better. Alright, guys, deep pooch left. Breakdown on Zach."

And Zach led them, "One, two, three," and then they all shouted in one voice, "War!"

As I watched them run out and line up for the kickoff, I felt a deep sense of pride in these young men and especially Zach, who had been such a good leader all year on special teams.

On Saguaro's first play from scrimmage after our kickoff, Brad Reisner recovered a fumble. Six plays later, on a field goal attempt by Cobb, Saguaro blocked it. We would later have a couple of extra points blocked, always by the same Saguaro player. Our offensive line coaches finally figured out what was happening. Ryan Sydnor, our right end, was blocking the man lined up in front of him instead of blocking down. That left a hole and a Saguaro player was sneaking up behind his teammate. Then when the ball was snapped he was bursting through the hole that Sydnor left, because he didn't block down toward the center.

Chaparral held again on defense and forced a punt. In just a few plays, the Firebirds had another touchdown on a QB sneak by Scott. The play before, he had hit Griffin on a pass down the middle to the one yard line. Griffin had fumbled, but Cobb had fallen on it at the one. It was now 28-0.

On Saguaro's next possession, Davey intercepted a pass at the Cats 37 yard line, after Ryan Sydnor, staying in his passing lane, had tipped the ball.

Three plays later, Scott hit Griffin in the left flat on a five yard out pattern and Griffin ran the final 10 yards into the end zone. 34-0.

Chaparral kicked off to start the third quarter. Saguaro picked up a first down, but after a sack by Brad Reisner, and another sack by Matt Kelley for 12 yards, the Sabercats were forced to punt.`

But they didn't punt. They ran a fake with the punter throwing a pass to one of his backs to his left. Josh Utterback, who in the Centennial game had left too early, played it right on the money! He had learned his lesson and tackled the receiver for a two yard loss. I gave him a high five as he came off the field after the play.

With the ball on the Saguaro 30, Scott threw an "out and up" to Griffin on the 13 yard line, and he broke a tackle on the three...and fell into the end zone for another touchdown. It was now 40-0.

On Saguaro's next possession, they punted from their 20 and with tremendous pressure from our punt block team, the punter just barely got the ball off. It went out of bounds on their 27—a seven yard punt.

The punt block team had scored a TD and set up two other TD's with their aggressive rush. This time Jerry scored from the one yard line, literally upending a tackler on the goal line. Jerry was back! 46-0.

Yes, there was one more touchdown. Davey scored from the nine yard line on *34 belly*. Final score, 53-0.

In a strange statistical twist, it was Chaparral's worst offensive game of the year, with the running game only picking up 112 yards and the passing game 153 yards, on seven for eight passes by Scott. He also threw three touchdown passes, two to Griffin and one to Cobb. Total offense–only 265 yards.

The big statistics were made by the defense. They held Saguaro to 96 yards rushing on 42 attempts and Brigham to 69 yards on 19 carries. Dobson was only six for 14 and 41 yards. Their total offense was only 137 yards, with three turnovers and a blocked punt. Chaparral's defense had registered their first shut-out of the year with Austin Sendlein 17, Jake Ireland 16, Matt Willden 15, and Brad Reisner leading the way with 10 tackle points, a sack and a fumble recovery.

We were to play the next game against the Nogales, Coconino winner. We had seen Coconino on tape, when they had played Apache Junction, and we thought that they were going to be tough. They were favored over Nogales.

That night, after the Saguaro game when we got to Ruby Tuesday's, we were surprised to find out Nogales had won 52-36. As we were soon to find out, Nogales ran their offense out of a shotgun and they had a quarterback who could put points on the scoreboard in a hurry. We had never faced anything quite like this before. Could the overcoming lessons the Firebirds had learned serve them well in this situation? Little did we know just how shell-shocked we would be at halftime, from Nogales' magnum firepower.

CHAPTER FOURTEEN

"SCARED TO DEATH"

I only knew one thing about Nogales. I had seen them play against Sabino in a passing league game at the University of Arizona, in a tournament there, the previous spring.

The two teams were a study in contrasts. Sabino was the top 4-A program in Tucson and usually ranked in the top three teams in the State at the beginning of each season. They had over 35 players dressed in similar shorts and shirts, looking very sharp and professional. By way of contrast, Nogales was dressed in different outfits. They looked like "Terry and the Pirates," but boy, could they ever play "pass" and "catch".

They beat Sabino that day in their 7 on 7 touch passing game, and when the game ended their team shouted as one and joined together in the middle of the field in a wild celebration, acting as though they had just won the Super Bowl.

There was a big crowd watching the game that day and most of the spectators joined in the fun and cheered the obvious underdog, Nogales, as they slayed the Goliath of 4-A Arizona football.

As I was riding home that night I thought to myself, *what a wonderful game this game of football really is. And what a great way to train young warriors. Those Nogales kids are a great example of what we call heart and overcoming adversity.*

Dana Zupke was concerned about Nogales' passing attack, especially out of their shotgun formation. This formation is configured by having the quarterback stand six yards behind the center, instead of right behind him. The strategy behind this formation enables the QB to have a better look at his receivers and gives him more time to throw the ball. Nogales' line, which looked more like a college line than a high school one, was the biggest line that we would face all year. It gave their QB, Roger Fontes, great protection. Fontes, who was 6'4" tall, was not only a very good passer, but he could run with the ball when he was forced out of the pocket.

Nogales had run their shotgun formation about 50% of the time in their previous three games, which we had seen on tape. What we didn't know was that they were planning on running that formation against us 90% of the time. They were going to run the ball just enough to keep our defense honest.

Matt Way thoughtfully watched the Nogales tape during the week, and commented that they were a decent team with a very good quarterback and a good receiver, Gilbert Tovar. He talked about their "speedy backs" and the "biggest offensive line he had ever seen." What Matt saw on the field was a different story! "Not only were they the biggest team, but the best team that we played all year," he would say after the game. "Shoot! I thought the Cactus team were the size of redwood trees–the Nogales line was even bigger."

Jake and Jerry were "gung ho" as usual. The entire week prior they kept repeating that we had to win this game to keep the train on the track.

For Clay and Goody, it took them a half to turn their effort up a notch. And they did!

This quarter-final game was played at 7:00 PM, Friday night, at a neutral field–Dobson High School, which was located in Mesa, about thirty minutes away from Chaparral. For some reason the field was wet, and it seemed to affect both teams, especially the running backs. Nogales, located south of Tucson on the Mexican border, had brought a large crowd with them, including their band. This was a huge game for them. They had never gotten this far in

176

the Playoffs before. Their energy was sky high, and they wanted to keep playing.

Chaparral won the toss and elected to receive. In all 12 games, we had either won the toss, or if the other team did, they had elected to receive in the second half, so that in every one of our games we received the opening kickoff. Winning the toss seemed to be a good omen for us.

If we won the toss, Ron always chose to take the ball first. He wanted his offense on the field as quickly as possible.

Griffin caught the kickoff on his five and made a good return, running to his left all the way back to our 35 yard line, almost breaking it all the way.

After a penalty on the first play, Jerry ran *33 belly* for 16 yards, running hard like the pre-injury Jerry. It was heartening to see him back in form and our sideline responded with cheers of encouragement. He had only gained 18 yards in six carries in the previous game against Saguaro, and had looked a little tentative (except on his TD run, when he had knocked over the tackler at the goal line).

First down. Cobb for seven yards on *45 power*.

Second down. *27 pitch* to Griffin around left end for four yards.

First down. Jerry on *33 belly*, the good old standby, for 11 yards.

First down. *28 sweep* by Griffin for 33 yards to the Nogales five yard line. Nogales' fast backs were having trouble catching our speedy Griffin.

First down. Bies was in for Griffin now, leading Jerry behind Clay's and Mike Reisner's block for a touchdown. In six plays Chaparral had moved the ball smoothly down the field for 65 yards and a TD. 7-0.

On Scott Lane's kickoff, the Nogales returner was hit hard on his 25. The ball popped out, Austin Sendlein picked it up and ran to the seven yard line. As he came off the field, he grinned impishly. "Sorry, coach," he told me, "I know you wanted a touchdown."

I cuffed him playfully on the shoulder, "That's okay, Austin. Great job." The kids knew that I loved to score touchdowns on special teams plays.

On first down, Scott ran *33 belly option* to his left. But it's not really an option. We don't want tacklers hitting our QB, so we tell Scott to fake the ball to Jerry, then pitch quickly to Cobb. Scott didn't look at Cobb. After the fake to Jerry, he ran the ball himself to the four yard line. And what we didn't want to happen...happened. He got hit and sprained his ankle as he went down. We could not afford to lose Scott. He seemed to be moving on it alright, with just a slight limp as he returned to the huddle. Not having an experienced QB ready as a back up, meant that he had to continue to play on that slightly sprained ankle.

It's not like the pro's where you can go to the "waiver wire" and pick up a player, or sign a free agent. You play with what you've got. In an emergency Ron would have played our JV quarterback, Ryan Benscoter, or Ryan Cobb, who had practiced at QB. After we scored, David, our trainer, taped up Scott's ankle. Scott played the rest of the game.

Second down. *26 power* and Griffin lost a yard.

Third down. We needed a score. Ron called *71*, a slant to our wide receiver, John Hogue. Scott, on his bad ankle, threw a perfect pass to Hogue. Hogue, with the defender all over his back, made a good catch for the TD. 14-0.

In less than four minutes and a total of nine offensive plays, we had scored two touchdowns. Maybe the two scores came a little too easy, because Nogales came back and scored three touchdowns on us, in the first half, without us scoring again.

On Nogales' first possession, it took them five plays to score. Their great wide receiver, Tovar (who would catch 11 passes for 180 yards) made a diving catch for 30 yards, and then caught another 30 yard pass over Larry Zak for a TD.

It was the first long pass that Larry had given up since the Centennial game. Larry always seemed to have a black hole over on his side of the field at right cornerback. If you threw long on him, the ball would be incomplete, falling into the black hole of the Bermuda Triangle out there. We had fun kidding Larry about that, but it was a great compliment to his defensive technique.

Larry was only 5'8", 170 pounds and ran the 40 in 4.8, but he had great pride in doing his job well. 14-7, Chaparral.

On the Nogales kickoff, Cobb caught the ball at the two, and running hard, returned the ball to our 31.

First down. Scott hit Jerry in the flat on *47 waggle* for 13 yards and a first down. Scott was limping noticeably now.

First down. *24 counter* and Griffin picked up four yards.

On second down, Jerry ran *34 belly* to the Nogales 43, but was tackled on a "cut tackle"– this is when a defensive back, instead of tackling with his arms and shoulders, rolls at the ball carrier's feet. It is dangerous for both players. We had not seen Nogales use this tackling technique when we reviewed their three previous games on tape.

We speculated that because of the way our four, hard running backs ran over defensive backs, that maybe Nogales had adopted this technique for this particular game. Jerry, especially with his braced knee, did not like it.

On fourth and one, on the Nogales 29, Cobb was stopped short on *47 sweep.*

The momentum had now swung to Nogales, as their defense joyfully left the field and the enthusiastic Nogales fans were on their feet clapping and shouting encouragement to their team.

It took Nogales seven plays to move the ball 71 yards for a touchdown. They had been throwing short passes on outs, hitches, and flanker screens. On our 24 yard line, Fontes threw the ball behind the line of scrimmage to one of his wide receivers. He caught the ball, and then instead of running upfield, threw a pass to his tight end, Coronado, running across the field.

It was a perfect pass, and the Chaparral secondary was fooled.

They missed the extra point and it was 14-13, favor of Chaparral.

Cobb returned the kickoff and exploded up to the Chaparral 41. But again Nogales held on downs on the Nogales 40.

On their first offensive play, Camello, who had never gotten beat deep by a wide receiver, almost picked off a pass on a deep out pattern. But Nogales was on a roll now, and in nine plays they had another TD, when Fontes rolled to his left and hit his receiver in the end zone, right between Zak and Willden, who were in a zone coverage.

Nogales went for two on the extra point. Fontes ran around with plenty of time to throw, but Chaparral had good coverage and the pass was incomplete. 19-14, Nogales.

On the last play of the half, Nogales tried a hook pass and then a lateral to another receiver, who was running behind the man who caught the ball. He fumbled and Camello recovered it on our 20 yard line.

The first half had been a disaster for us. We couldn't stop their passing game, and couldn't seem to get any pressure on Fontes. He had 187 yards in the first half alone. We were shell-shocked as we went into the locker room.

It was going to be a long, sad bus ride back to Chaparral High School unless we found some way to shut down Fontes and his receivers. The coaches were scratching their heads, mentally mulling over strategy, and feeling they had been shot full of gunshot holes when we gathered together.

But not the kids! The kids seemed to be confident...more so than the coaches. Perhaps their confidence came from seeing the coaching staff never panic–just quietly go about their business of making adjustments. There were times, however, when we were relieved they didn't have x-ray vision.

We made a couple of adjustments, but the major one was made by Coach Zupke when he changed the right linebackers' responsibilities. He had Matt Way or David Williams, whoever was in there, rush the QB from *his* left side. Since he was left-handed, he would run to his left when pressure came, because it was easier to throw on the run to his left than to his right. We noticed that when he ran to his right, he floated the ball and it gave our defensive backs more time to get to the ball. But when Fontes ran to his left, he threw bullet passes. It was an acute and highly strategic observation by Coach Zupke. We hoped by adjusting to this tendency of Fontes, that we could roll up the tanks and howitzers to counter the magnum force which was shooting us down.

We kicked off to start the second half. After 10 plays, Nogales was on our 15 getting ready to score again and put this game out of reach. But then, the defense came up with two big plays.

On third down, the center snapped the ball a little high. Fontes had trouble holding on to it. By the time he picked it up, Matt Kelley and Sendlein were all over him like a collapsing circus tent. They threw him for a 15 yard loss back to the 30.

On fourth down, Mike Camello made a great play, knocking a pass away from Tovar on a deep out pattern.

We took over on our own 30. We needed a score badly to get the momentum swinging over our way.

First down. *33 belly* for four.

Second down. Scott completed an out pattern to Griffin for six yards and a first down.

First down. Jerry ran *32 trap* for five yards and got "cut tackled" again. It bothered his knee and Davey replaced him.

31 trap for no gain on second down.

Third and third. Big down. We needed a first down here to keep the drive going. Ron called *45 power* and behind Jake and Davey's blocks, Cobb ran hard for 15 yards to the Nogales 40. There was a collective sigh of relief on our sidelines as our fans roared in the stands behind us.

First down. *32 trap* and Davey got four tough yards before being tackled. We had the running game going now. Good rhythm.

Now, Ron fooled the Nogales defense by calling *33 belly pass,* where Scott fakes to Davey and steps back in the pocket. It freezes the defensive back covering John Hogue, just long enough for Hogue to get behind him. Scott, on his gimpy ankle, threw a perfect pass—air mailed it straight to Hogue. He was finally tackled on the four yard line. It was the turning point in the game.

On the next play, Scott quick pitched to Cobb, running to his right, on *48 pitch.* Cobb sprinted to the right corner of the end zone for a TD. 20-19. The extra point was blocked.

On the sidelines I said, "Dana, same thing as Saguaro—Sydnor didn't block down again."

Nogales had seen the Saguaro film and obviously were trying the same tactics as Saguaro on extra points.

"Let's put Sendlein in place of Sydnor next time," I suggested.

But it was Dana's call. He had the responsibility for the offensive line.

"No, Sydnor is going to do it right," he told me.

And as Sydnor came off the field Dana was in his face making sure that Ryan did it right. And after that, Ryan did. We had
no more problems that night on extra points. But we still had problems.

After the kick off, Nogales started on their 25. Chaparral ur-
gently needed a defensive stop. The words, "Don't let Nogales
back in the game!" circled in my mind like a mantra.

After several plays, which included a sack, the defense forced
Nogales to punt...finally! It was the only time all night that Nogales
would punt.

As usual, the punt block team revved up the pressure cooker,
almost blocking it. Griffin returned it to our 44 yard line.

First down. We needed a score. We needed some breathing
room–20-19 wasn't much of a lead against this offensive machine.
Adam Goodworth punched Jerry lightly on the shoulder, "Hurry
up and score and get your job done," he told him.

Griffin picked up nine yards on *26 power*.

Jerry ran for no gain on second down, running *32 trap*.

Third down. Another big down. I had told Ron a few plays
before that I thought *44 blast pass* to Jerry would be wide open. I
seldom venture the suggestion of a certain play I think will work,
although he encourages me to do so. He has good help upstairs on
the phones in Jim Ellison and his assistant Lenny Abt. Also, Ron
is tremendously focused when we have the ball and is incisively
effective in his play calling.

I only suggest a play if I am sure that, first of all he hasn't
thought of it, and secondly, that the defense is doing, or not doing, something that he doesn't know about. In this particular instance I had noticed that when we lined up in our slot formation;
that is, a back lined up between our split end and tackle (rather
than on a wing, one yard outside our tight end), that Nogales had

only one defender outside our tight end on the other side, and that the flat was wide open.

On *44 blast pass*, Scott fakes the ball to Cobb on a quick hand off (blast) and then takes a quick step back and hits Jerry in the backfield. Then it's Jerry one-on-one if there is a defensive back there.

Ron called the play, and on this particular play, because there was no defender, (the defensive end had come across the line on the blast fake) Jerry went across the line of scrimmage. Scott smartly held the ball a little bit longer and waited for Jerry to turn his head. As soon as he did, Scott put a nice touch on the pass right into Jerry's hands. He ran it all the way to the 21 yard line, where he got cut tackled, again.

As Jerry limped off the field, Davey replaced him at fullback. On the first play, *34 belly*, Davey, running behind the right side of the line, scored from 21 yards out.

Ellie Davis and Jake executed a perfect crossblock at the point of attack, and Cobb led through the hole that sprung Davey for the TD. Cobb kicked the all important extra point. 27-19.

No one was relaxed on our sideline, not as long as the ever dangerous Fontes was throwing the ball.

On our kick off, Scott Lane kicked a perfect long pooch to the 15, and when the returner finally picked it up on our left sideline, he was swarmed at the 18 yard line. They had poor field position.

After a first down on their 33, Fontes was rushed hard by Goody. Goody dove, but missed the tackle. Then, our other end, Matt Kelley, missed a tackle. Now Fontes was running loose up the middle of the field like a runaway horse with the bit in his teeth. There was no one in front of him.

It looked like a big gainer, but a hand reached out from behind him and knocked the ball loose. Fontes had not seen the ever-hustling Chris Dobbins as he reached in and hit the ball. It hit the ground–Davey Williams was on the alert–he fell on it. Our crowd went wild. It was a huge play.

On first down, Griffin took the ball on *28 sweep*, found a hole and cut it back to the middle of the field. He crossed the end zone untouched...a 33 yard run.

Cobb kicked the extra point. 34-19.

Willden intercepted a pass on Nogales' next possession and it was over.

Everybody, fans, players and coaches gave a huge sigh of relief. Nogales had given us the scare of our lives, at least for this season. The first Saguaro game was tough for us when we were behind 17-0 at halftime. But we felt that we could stop Saguaro.

We weren't really sure at halftime against Nogales that we could stop them. Fontes was the best quarterback that we had played against this season. We wished him luck at whatever college he would play for next year. We were just glad that we didn't have to play him again!

Nogales' passing game had gained 290 yards, a staggering amount, on 19 for 36 passes and three TD's. We had held their running game to 47 yards on 23 carries, for a two yard average. Our defense had three fumble recoveries and an intercepted pass.

Matt Willden had 17 tackle points, Mike Camello 12 (when your defensive backs lead the team, you know that you've been in trouble), and Sendlein, Bies, Matt Way and Mike Reisner all had 11.

On offense, Griffin had another great game, gaining 114 yards on 11 carries for a 10.4 yard average and a TD. Jerry had 107 yards on 17 carries and a TD, for a 6.3 yard average. Davey had 23 yards on two carries and a TD. Cobb had 42 yards on eight carries and a TD, and Hogue had two big catches–one for a TD, and one that set up a TD. Scott played a courageous game on his bad ankle and passed 6 for 11 and 86 yards with one TD.

The atmosphere on the bus ride home was one of euphoria laced with relief. When we got to Ruby Tuesday's, we found that our semi-final opponent would be Mingus.

The next Friday, November 28, 1997, Darren Urban heightened the excitement for the 4A State football semifinal and profiled several of our players. His astute predictions had an uncanny track record of being right on target. Could we live up to his prediction: "Chaparral 34, Mingus 27"?

Just one more game until the Championship game at Sun Devil Stadium. Everyone began saying, "Just one more game"...

CHAPTER FIFTEEN

"MINGUS–THE SEMIFINAL GAME"

And so the season had rolled forward through mountain top wins, and the rich soil of problem valleys to be overcome. By sinking their cleats into the soggy turf of obstacles, the Firebirds had risen to the challenge of conquering the handicap of player loss due to injuries. They had plugged the holes, risen to the top. Now, could they keep the momentum going for this one more game against Mingus?

As John Kriekard, principal, and his wife, Janie, drove down from their home in the McDowell mountains that night, as the vibrant sunset brushed muted color across the canvas of the sky, one thought predominated: "Just one more game"...

And as Sam and Kim Schwartzberg drove toward the game, worrying if the brace on Jerry's knee would impede his performance, their thoughts centered on the same thing. Sam had squeezed her hand saying, "Just one more game."

While Cindi Muschinski headed for the game, believing in her heart, Clay's deceased father would somehow be watching, she too had repeated the thought, "Just one more game."

In spite of Darren Urban's prediction of a Chaparral victory, the coaching staff was nervous. Primarily, we were concerned about the physical health of the team. Scott Johnson had not been able to practice all week because of his sprained ankle. He intended to play and we were hoping that our running game would dominate Mingus, so that we wouldn't need to pass.

Larry Zak, our predictably consistent cornerback, had sprained his ankle during practice on Monday–he was out of the game. Clay Muschinski, Jake Ireland and Chris Dobbins were all nursing injuries that limited their practice time. I tried to ward off thoughts the team seemed to be jinxed by the "sprain god." Taking a "Mash unit" to the game as mascot might have been appropriate.

Although Jerry was running hard, it was obvious that the brace on his knee had cut down and almost eliminated his explosiveness, especially when he changed directions in the open field. And if anybody had told us before the game that we would lose Josh Griffin in the second half with a serious hand injury, we would have been even more concerned than we already were.

The second thing we worried about was the Mingus team itself. They were well coached, and their offense could really put points on the board. They had a big offensive line, two outstanding running backs, both of whom had gained over 1,000 yards. Their quarterback had great accuracy when he threw the long ball.

Their offense had scored over 150 points in their past three games, and when we watched Mingus on film, we realized that their quarterback, Ryan Stokes, was a great athlete who could dodge on-rushing linemen and give his receivers more time to get open. Mike Rohrer, their leading rusher, was also a dangerous receiver coming out of the backfield.

Dana Zupke worked hard with his defense all week to cover Rohrer and their fullback, on pass patterns where they try to get matched up against slower linebackers.

It was game time–7 o'clock, Friday night at Shadow Mountain High School, a neutral site for the semi-final playoff game. The stands were jam packed and fans numbering about 5,000 spilled into the overflow on both sides of the field. The crisp night air and high tension of the crowd served to heighten the crackling excitement.

The Mingus Marauders kicked off to open the game, and in the first offensive series, Griffin ran *24 counter* 76 yards for a touchdown. Cobb missed the extra point. 6-0. Sensational start!

On Mingus' first series the Firebird defense held them and forced a punt. In what proved to be an ominous omen for this game, Jake broke through the line and got there so quickly that the punt went underneath his hands. He hit the punter, knocking him down. It was a 15 yard penalty and a first down for Mingus. Our defense held them on the 23 yard line, and their kicker, Wilcox, kicked a 40 yard field goal. 6-3.

The Marauders defense held us, and then, on a third down play, Stokes hit Jon Carillo down the left sideline for 38 yards to our 25 yard line. Stokes scored, from one yard out, a few plays later. The extra point was good, and it was 10-6, Mingus.

Chaparral came back with a long drive that ended in a touchdown when Scott hit Cobb on an out and up for 15 yards. We missed the extra point, and it was now 12-10, Chaparral. The crowd would surely have collective laryngitis on Saturday. The closeness of the score which seesawed back and forth seemed to light a bonfire of excitement under the fans.

After the kickoff, with Mingus on their own 33, and 43 seconds left in the half, Stokes, under pressure from Adam Goodworth, managed to get off a long pass to the speedy Rohrer. Rohrer took it all the way to the end zone for a 67 yard touchdown. It was a spectacular climax to the half. With a two point conversion, it made the score 18-12, Mingus.

The large contingent from Cottonwood, who had come to the valley from the mountains, erupted. In contrast, the Chaparral bench and their fans became unusually quiet. The quick strike by Mingus, just before the half, had deflated the Chaparral quiet confidence that had carried them through their many previous battles.

At halftime, coaches Estabrook and Zupke went through their usual adjustment period. For coach Zupke, the big concern was the Mingus backs slipping out and running deep pass patterns, which put their speed against our slower safeties.

Mingus took the second half kickoff and marched 71 yards, all on running plays, for a touchdown that put them up 24-12.

Stokes scored on a six yard rollout. They were stopped on their two point conversion try.

Mingus' defense stopped us and on their next drive, Stokes again found Rohrer on third and 14 for a 46 yard TD pass. The two point conversion was good and it was 32-12. It seemed to be slipping through our fingers.

But then, Scott Johnson, playing courageously on his gimpy ankle, led a drive where Chris Medill, who had replaced the injured Griffin, scored from nine yards out on *28 sweep*. It was 32-18, as we missed our two point conversion.

We tried an onside kick, but Mingus recovered it and marched 60 yards for their last TD of the night. They kicked the extra point and it was 39-18.

Our kids weren't through yet. They showed the stuff of champions as they got another drive going, and this time Jerry scored from three yards out. 39-24, Mingus.

Adam Goodworth beamed and gave Jerry a "high five" after the touchdown. "Jerry, I love you." he yelled hoarsely, "Even if this is the last TD for us together...I love you!"

This time, on our kickoff, Jake recovered the onside kick by Scott Lane. There were six minutes left in the game. We still had a chance...

On the first play from scrimmage, Scott threw a long pass to Cobb, who was open on the Mingus 10 yard line, but it was just a little short and the Mingus defender tipped it away. That drive finally ended on their ten yard line, when we couldn't convert on fourth down. Final score 39-24, Mingus.

It was over–and also over were our hopes of going to Sun Devil Stadium. Somehow it just didn't seem possible. After winning every single game in the season, the defeat was crushing at the end of the game. Our kids had played their hearts out, but we just got beat. No excuses.

In spite of the score we had more first downs than Mingus, and more rushing yards. We had 292 rushing yards to their 200. We had 8.2 yards per carry to their 4.6 yards per carry. Griffin had gained 163 yards on 10 carries, before he got hurt, for an unbelievable 16.3 yard average. Jerry had 100 yards in 17 carries for a 5.9 yard average. Scott threw 33 times, completing 15 passes for 195 yards, with one TD, and one costly interception. Cobb caught five passes for 41 yards, and Goody caught five passes for 80 yards.

Mingus had made the big plays though, and it was reflected in the statistics. Stokes had only attempted nine passes–he completed five of these. Four of those were key third down plays. If we had stopped those third down passes, Mingus would have been forced to punt. The only non-third down pass that Stokes completed, was on the first down pass to Rohrer, just before the half, for 67 yards and a T.D. Stokes' five pass completions were for an unbelievable 190 yards.

Stokes and Rohrer were "big-play guys," just as we had expected. We just didn't expect them to be that successful. Rohrer ended up with 109 yards rushing and 119 yards from three pass receptions.

Coach Estabrook had gotten some second guessing from fans, who asked why we had passed so much in the second half when we had such a powerful and effective running game. His answer was put very simply: "When you are down three touchdowns, in order to catch up, you have to lengthen the game, and by passing even an incompletion stops the clock."

And we had our chances, an interception down near the Mingus goal line stopped one drive, and if the tipped pass to Cobb had been a little longer, we would have been right back in the game. Football and its strategy make it a great sport to second guess, but Ron would not have done it differently if he had it to do over again.

My heart went out to the players, who could not hide their disappointment, and I felt sympathetic toward the parents who had pinned their hopes on "just one more game." I searched the stands for the Schwartzbergs, the Ways, Alan and Irene Goodworth, Cindi Muschinski. Some had sought each other out...talking...consoling...re-hashing.

Now, Ron gathered a tearful group of kids together at one end of the field. We could hear the war hoops and hollering of the

Mingus team from the other end of the field. We now knew how the twelve other teams we had played that season had felt.

Ron repositioned his tinted glasses with one finger. "We got beat tonight," he told them. "But it doesn't take away from what you've accomplished this year. We are 12 and 1, the best record a Chaparral High School football team has ever had."

Jake Ireland lightly cuffed Jerry on the shoulder. There were several solemn nods around the circle of players. Two of the JV team gave each other rather dejected "high fives." It reminded me more of when my babies had played pattycake, than the vigorous enthusiastic slapping it usually signaled.

"No other team in the history of the school has made it to the semi-finals before," Ron continued. "You should be proud of yourselves for what you've accomplished. Don't let this loss ruin what has been a great experience for all of us." Ron had put everything in its rightful place.

It wasn't the end of the world. It *was* the end of a dream, but it was important for these young men, who were no longer kids, to put this game in the proper perspective of what they had accomplished together over this past year.

The game of life–not the game of football–is really the championship. The lessons learned in teamwork, overcoming, assuming responsibility over the past season, would carry them to the real championship played out in the future. And yes, hard as it is to take at the time, sometimes defeat is a part of the pattern which develops true character.

Darren Urban's column bore the headline, "Banged up Firebirds Go Down Fighting." This was one game that, try as hard as they could, adversity just would not be overcome.

As the Mingus coach was to say later, "They (Chaparral) never quit. We thought that we had them down and out a couple of times, but they just kept coming back."

This is a quality of great warriors–that they never quit. In a quiet time of sober thinking I realized I would have opted to go to war with any one of these young men.

I wanted to talk with the team individually–get into their minds to find out just what they had learned over the year, find out what impact the season had on them. The weight training program had built up their bodies. Had we made a difference in their lives, as Red Caughron, my high school coach, had in my life?

CHAPTER SIXTEEN

"FROM THE FOOTBALL BANQUET
TO LIFE'S BANQUET"

The football banquet that celebrated the season's end for the three teams, freshmen, junior varsity and varsity, was a bittersweet occasion. It was sweet in a sense of profound accomplishment for the freshman team under its head coach, Nick DeMember, who had gone 8-0, sweet for the junior varsity 7-1, and sweet for the varsity, 12-1.

For the 350 people who came to honor these young men, it was an affirmation of Dr. Kriekard's theme of "excellence." That was the "sweet" aspect. The bitter part was that this was the last time we would be with the seniors as a team–as a family.

I remember standing with Matt Willden and Ryan Cobb after the banquet was over. Ryan said, "This is so sad...it's over." And it hit me also.

"You're right, Ryan," I told him. "It was a unique, once-in-a-lifetime experience. I'm sure going to miss you guys." We hugged.

I woke up the next day still sad and a bit depressed. It continued for the rest of the week. And, in talking with the players later, and the other coaches, there was shared sadness and a sense of loss.

Truthfully, there was also disappointment in losing to Mingus. Mingus had a sensational team that kept getting better each week, and it beat Sabino in the Championship game at Sun Devil Stadium 23-14. All of us, coaches and players, felt that we played our worst game of the year, but Mingus had honed their skills, played well, and deserved to win. It boiled down to the fact that they just played better than we did. They merited the win.

There was more than just a feeling of disappointment, though. We had been a family–a team–a group of people who had put the team first and their own individual agendas second. In attempting to search my own feelings, I realized with a startling revelation that it was similar to the death of a close friend. I was in mourning.

We had experienced so much together which strengthened the bond of closeness. The overcoming ingredient had seemed to weld the cohesive quality between us. It was not just the factor of having to come from behind together, but the factors of suffering collectively through Jerry's injury, plus watching Scott persevere through a frustrating first half of the season. There were the injuries many of the players had to rise above. It had been important for each person to do their job, make their contribution for the good of the whole, not let the team down.

Lessons learned through this period would form stepping stones to a rich legacy for the seniors to build on, the rest of their lives. In the future these young men would face many situations where they would have to employ overcoming skills in their jobs, churches, and raising families. The coaches firmly believed that the lessons learned from the game we call "football" can be applied for extra yardage in their lives–earned points in the game of life.

The team seemed to trace their cohesive bonding back to the first week of camp at San Diego State. At the end of practice when they ran sprints for conditioning, they began pushing each other by shouting encouragement, motivating and urging on other team members. They tried to inspire confidence and these ingredients carried over into the season itself. They never got down on each other, but rather, inspired and uplifted each other. From an adult perspective, it was easy to see that these important lessons helped them to overcome the many adversities.

The senior members of the team were more than just football players, and this story would not be complete without talking about each one of them. You, the reader, should be able to see them as individuals–unique human beings, who grew in many ways over that particular twelve months when the odyssey first began.

When I think of Scott Johnson, I don't think about all the school records that he set. I frankly reflect on his perseverance, his demeanor laced with a sense of class, which seemed to be a signature of his personality. The first half of the season he was not a big part of the offensive statistics, but without his leadership, we would not have been successful.

During that period of time, I was with Scott during our offensive group period as he would throw passes to our receivers. Each day that went by I would say, "Okay, Scotter, let's go," and he would faithfully go do his job. He never pouted–he never complained that we were not throwing the ball, as we had done in the two previous years. Because I had known him for over six years I could pretty well tell what he was thinking and feeling. It became an important part of my job to encourage him–every day. Coaching quarterbacks was not my responsibility, but encouraging every young man was.

I feel that encouragement is the most important single thing that we do as coaches, in working with young men. The word "encourage" in Greek literally means, "to impart courage."

Our coaching staff has a phrase that we have incorporated into our coaching philosophy, "praise, correct, praise." We are not into the marine corps sergeant type of coaching. For instance, if one of my receivers drops a pass, I might say, "Nice pattern, but the reason that you dropped the ball was you didn't catch it with your fingers. Good effort though."

Scott overcame–overcame the friction with Coach Estabrook during the first part of the year. In fact, Ron was quoted in Darren Urban's column of November 20, 1997 as saying, "Looking at Scott Johnson's numbers...doesn't begin to show the 6' 3", 195 pounder's value."

"Why does everyone rate a quarterback strictly by his numbers? The true leader leads mentally, and physically, makes good judgments, help people with the blocking assignments, carries through with his fakes and hands the ball off well. It's about being a total quarterback. It's more than the statistics." Scott and the Coach overcame their initial rocky relationship.

He also overcame his own personal disappointment at not being involved more in the offense, and the friction that had been ongoing between his father and Coach Estabrook. But perhaps the largest hurdle to overcome was the painful ankle sprain he endured to play in the last two games. And when he was given the opportunity to pass more, beginning with the Apache Junction game, he grabbed it and was successful. Scott was a leader when it was not always easy to be a leader. If those lessons in overcoming that he has learned, are carried over to life, he is going to be a tremendously productive human being.

When I think back on Jerry Schwartzberg, I can't help but remember the number of things in addition to his many honors: second team All-State; and Player of the Year for the City of Scottsdale. I've never known anyone, male, female, young, or old who had the work ethic, with single mindedness of purpose, that this young man had. At halftime during the Apache Junction game, while the other coaches were meeting with their groups, I was with David McAdon, our trainer, and Doctor Fred Dicke as they attended to Jerry's injury. As tears of frustration poured down his cheeks, I felt helpless to say the right thing. There were no words of comfort available to me.

I didn't sleep much that night. The next morning, in our small training room, Jerry was sitting on the upraised table where David did his taping. Everyone else, except David, had left to go and jog with the team. Jerry seemed to be in better spirits that morning. There was no swelling, which the doctor indicated meant there had been no other damage to the knee other than the ACL.

"Jerry, how would you feel about my praying for you?" I asked. I felt so helpless, unable to do anything in my own power to make it right. I wondered how he'd receive my suggestion.

He sighed heavily. "Good...I'd like that." There was a resolve in the tone of his voice.

I had spoken to the Fellowship of Christian Athletes awhile ago. Jerry was a member so I had had a hunch my request would be well received. I laid my hands on his knee, praying silently.

Jerry seemed to view this injury as a test...another test to overcome. Well, he passed the test with flying colors, coming back to play courageously in the last couple of games. After the season, he had the required operation and rehabbed at "Jerry speed," which is warp speed–about twice as fast as the normal person.

The telephone stopped ringing from college recruiters after the injury so Jerry decided to "walk-on" at ASU and play football there. When Jerry sets his mind to something it's a done deal. I feel certain we will be reading about Jerry in the sports pages again.

Jake Ireland had proven his point. He overcame what he had termed a "sub-poor junior year." He knew that he was a better football player than what he had shown. He was on a mission. As it turned out, it was not "Mission Impossible." He accomplished making first team linebacker, All Conference and All-City. He also made second team All Conference offensive guard.

Jake was a big play guy, blocking two field goals and a punt that had dramatically affected all three games. He was the emotional leader of the team–and this was not an especially emotional team. There weren't many highs nor lows, just a consistent workmen-like attitude that sometimes was interpreted by the coaches as laid back. If something needed to be said on behalf of the team, Jake usually was the spokesman. His passion seemed to be football; he had an obvious love affair with it. Jake will play in a small college somewhere next year, loving every minute of it–romancing the game.

Matt Way made second team All-Conference, and second team All City at linebacker. His position coach, Scott Heideman, thought that he was the smartest and best linebacker in the conference. Matt was quiet, but an astute student of the game. He was never fooled on a counter, reverse or screen pass by the other team. He made it a practice to study and scrutinize tapes of the other team's games. This just seemed to be a part of his personal work ethic of always being ready–always prepared. It never seemed to occur to him that there was another way to get the job done. He will surely take those attributes into a successful future.

Although the above four young men were the co-captains of the team and well-suited for team leadership, there was also great leadership from the senior class and also from some juniors.

Clay Muschinski was one of those seniors. I had known Clay and his family for some years. His older brother, Corbin, was a friend of my son, Jed; they had played football together.

Clay had grown into a large, powerful young man, and was a well-rounded athlete playing both baseball and basketball on younger teams. He had made the All-Conference team as a sopho-more and now was one of the premier offensive linemen in the state making second team All-State, plus All Conference and All City. He had turned into a devastating blocker and was personally enthusiastic about the off-season weight lifting program. He told me after the season, "If these young guys (meaning freshmen and sophomores) keep lifting, with their great attitude, they're going to be super strong their senior year...and with their attitude..." His voice trailed off as he shook his head in obvious appreciation for the underclassmen.

Clay had a great sense of humor, but there was also a very serious flip side. To watch this young man mature over the past few years was a great pleasure discussed by all his coaches–behind his back, of course.

Adam Goodworth was the "renaissance man" of the team. He had made All City and All Conference at tight end for three years in a row. His long-haired renaissance exterior was not a facade, it was a deep part of the core of his nature. His vibrant intensity extended to many interests: an intellectual thirst which resulted in high scholastic standings; probing and diverse interests which ranged from plants and goldfish, to motorcycles, to deep spiritual beliefs.

If Adam asked a coach a question, which he frequently did, it was well thought out. And you'd better have an answer so that you wouldn't be embarrassed. Adam, who did not like to lift weights, was still in the weight room in April after the season was over. He had decided to attend the Colorado School of Mines in preparation for an engineering career, and play football there. He finally had come to admit how important the weight program was. Frankly, none of us ever thought we would see Adam in the weight room on his own initiative.

He will always be remembered as a leader, will always be a leader because he wears an obvious mantle of moral authority.

Chris Dobbins had made All-Conference at defensive tackle for the past two years. He was predictably consistent, always hustling, always pursuing the ball. There was a depth of constancy in his personality which seemed to dictate he was the same every day, practicing the same way that he played–all out, every day, every play. Most people don't have the fortitude to maintain that steady a course.

The Chaparral coaches were pleased that the other coaches in our conference appreciated Chris' qualities as much as we did. When voting for All-Conference came about each year, Ron Estabrook would nominate our players, but we could not vote for them. We were required to vote for our opponents players. Chris had a work ethic that was similar to Matt Way's. These were young men who gave you the same high effort consistently. What a wonderful attribute to have. I secretly wished it were possible to bottle it, and spoon it out in doses at the beginning of each football season.

Ryan Cobb, who made second team All-City receiver, was a player I was constantly with all year around. At Chaparral we have a year around kicking program. Ryan had never kicked before his senior year, so we had a lot of work to do in the off season. Ryan had a good season at running back his junior year, but we thought that he had the potential to be an All-State receiver. He was receptive to the idea of moving to receiver. Early in the season, however, when we weren't throwing much, he felt that he was not contributing to the team and became frustrated. He was moved to running back, and still ended up being our leading receiver. He not only had a great year, Ryan matured emotionally and physically, becoming a hard-nosed runner, and a very tough blocker. I think the thing I remember most about him is his comment responding to my announcement to him that he had been voted the All-Conference kicker. "That's hard to believe," he exclaimed. "I wasn't the best kicker, Rubino was." Ryan has a fresh openness and an honesty which we all came to appreciate.

Matt Kelley, who made first team All-Conference and second team All-City at defensive end, was the surprise package of our team his junior year. That year, before the season started, the coaching staff was thinking of recommending to him that he step down to the JV team and get some playing experience.

The staff was in for a shocking eye-opener. We were filming our team defensive period early in the season. During practice Coach John Reinhardt, the defensive line coach in 1996, kept noticing that there was only one defensive end who consistently performed his techniques correctly. It was Matt Kelley. What a pleasant surprise he had been.

And then, in this season, he quietly matured into a defensive end who ended up with the highest grade, game-after-game. He became the role model for every small, slow defensive lineman who is determined to play—willing to be "coachable."

In honor of Matt, we have an unofficial "Matt Kelley award," given to the player who surprises us the most by performing way beyond the coaches' expectations. Matt Kelley himself won the "Matt Kelley award" in this year.

David Williams would probably have been a first string running back at any other high school, but he had the misfortune of playing behind Jerry. When Jerry was injured, David stepped in and our running game didn't miss a beat. Jerry was faster and a harder runner than Davey, but Davey had great vision and was especially effective after he got through the line, read the blocks downfield and weaved his way toward the goal line.

Davey also did a great job at linebacker, was a standout on special teams, blocking punts, and was our long snapper on punts and extra points.

During his junior year I had been especially tough on him during a film session on Saturday morning—in fact, too tough. I made the remark that it appeared he was just standing around instead of getting the job done. It was belittling, in front of the other players, but instead of backing off, I continued to rag on him. It was uncalled for, without the uplifting praise which should have accompanied any critique.

I felt bad about it all weekend and then on the next Monday we happened to walk together out to the practice field. I put my arm around his shoulder and we talked about blocking a punt the next game, which he did. I think that he knew that my motivation was right and that I had just overdone it in trying to make him the best possible player that he could be. After that incident we had a very close player-coach relationship.

Matt Willden, who made second team All-Conference and All-City safety was under-rated. He had improved his speed in the 40 during the offseason from 5.1 to 4.6. He was a hard hitting tackler and an excellent cover man on passes. Matt also held for extra points, and except for one fumbled snap, handled all of the snaps for the kicker perfectly.

Being the holder on kicks is an extremely responsible position and not always appreciated. I was his position coach in offensive and defensive groups most of the year. My biggest nightmare was that the players would get tired of hearing my voice and tune me out. But Matt, Ryan Cobb and Larry Zak had continuous one-liners which livened things up. They always ragged on each other to keep Coach Dennis Riccio and me entertained. We had fun, and Matt made sure of that. Every day before practice, or whenever they saw me, Matt and Larry Zak would call out in sing-song voices, "Coach Mott...ley!" It was their special trademark and it was their way of greeting me every day.

Matt plans on going to Brigham Young University and being a doctor someday.

Larry Zak, who made honorable mention All-Conference and All-City as cornerback, was another under-rated cornerback. He only got beat deep twice all year, in 13 games. That's got to be some sort of record in itself.

Two specific instances stand out vividly in my mind regarding Larry. It happened in the Nogales game. Larry had gotten beaten for a TD early in the game, and had trouble in the first half tackling their quick, slippery receivers after they caught the short passes. Just before the half, I replaced him with Chris Medill. I was watching him closely when he came off the field. If he hung his head and wouldn't look at me, I knew that his confidence was shot; he'd probably be through for the rest of the game. But he wasn't hanging his head. There was fire in his eyes–he wanted back in the game. It was the reaction I was looking for, and he had a great second half. Also, putting more pressure on their QB helped make his job a little bit easier.

The other instance I remember put pressure on *me*. At practice one day I made the mistake of saying something about a "half-assed effort"–I can't even remember now what I was referring to, but Larry and Matt Willden called me on it immediately.

"Coach Mottley," Larry said, "We've never heard you cuss before." A sly smile spread across his face. Matt was already grinning.

I had been on them about their language at times and was caught in the cross hairs of their backfire. "The word 'ass' is not cussing," I told them rather facetiously, "it means a 'donkey'." But all three of us knew they had me dead to rights, and they never let me hear the end of it. I learned a lesson, needless to say, I never used the word "ass" again–at least not on school grounds.

Ryan Sydnor played defensive end for us for two years and was Adam Goodworth's backup at tight end. The two of them were close best friends. I think that being able to practice together made practices easier for both of them.

Ryan was a quiet, conscientious young man who had a twinkle of mischief in his eyes when kidded. He and Matt Kelley were key to making our defense work, and Ryan just got better and better as the season progressed. We always had a lot of fun in our tight end receiving drills. Adam, Ryan and Austin Sendlein made a concerted effort every practice to convince me that they had the best hands on the team, and that all the passes thrown during a game should always be directed to the tight ends.

The other seniors, Bobby Gersten, and Jeff O'Connor, didn't get on the field much, but they were important to the team. Jeff, our excellent discus thrower on the track team, had transferred from Arcadia in his junior year.

In the Arcadia game, playing for Chaparral in his senior year, he blocked a punt against them. He was obviously excited to contribute a final one-two punch to his ex-school. Jeff and Bobby both contributed to the special teams in both their junior and senior years.

The sequel to this book is in the hands of the returning juniors and sophomores, and of course, that ball is in the court of Coach Ron Estabrook, whom I sat down with after the season was over. Ron had orchestrated THE TURNAROUND, and while I had witnessed every twist and turn in the road to success, I was eager and curious to pick his brain further—scratch the fertile soil which had allowed stellar players to blossom from the sod of a football field.

"What are the ingredients that made this season so successful?" I asked him. "It obviously didn't happen without a plan by you, Ron. What was the plan?"

His eyes narrowed as he stared into the distance. The hint of a smile flickered across his face, as though he fleetingly savored some memory. "There are three ingredients—three groups, actually, that make a successful high school football program. Those three groups need to work in harmony, and the people in those groups need to feel good about each other."

"Three groups?" I'd expected him to lay out some hard-hitting formula for building players.

"Those three groups, each separate and distinct, are the ingredients, Chuck, and they must respect the role each has to play. Two out of three won't get the job done."

I could feel lines of puzzlement furrowing into my forehead.

"The first necessary ingredient is the support of the school administration. The administration, led by a principal who believes strongly that extra curricular activities are as important in the high school experience as academics, is paramount.

"Football is simply one of those activities, but because of its nature and timing, it has a major impact on any high school campus. It is the first school activity of the new school year."

I nodded in agreement.

"It sets the tone for the whole school year–the socialization–the teamwork concept–the commitment, spirit, participation and creates a general attitude that is carried over into all aspects of a young person's life. We want everyone involved in our program to have a strong commitment to it, to feel good about each other, and to have fun. The adminstration's support is so important because that attitude of strong backing passes down to all school employees."

I began to see where Ron was going with this.

"The second necessary ingredient is the group of the Coaching Staff and Players. As you know, we have 14 coaches on staff–four each on Junior Varsity and Freshman teams, six on the Varsity. I try to hire coaches who have the same philosophy that I do in coaching young men."

"That's obvious," I told him. "All of us meld together well for that reason."

"I believe in establishing a system, and installing that same system at all three levels–Freshman, Junior Varsity and Varsity, and then being consistent in staying with it. And of course, it goes without saying, that the weight training program is key...having players commit to it on a year around basis, starting in the summer before their Freshman year."

He traced the wet ring, left by his bottle of water, with one finger and said thoughtfully, "Commitment by the players to the program creates an ownership in the program by them, Chuck, which in turn, creates a family atmosphere. Part of my goal is to carry over that same attitude to the classroom. As you know, I carefully monitor each player's academic program also."

I nodded again and remembered all the things Coach Estabrook had instituted at Chaparral which helped create a family atmosphere. T-shirts with slogans on them flashed momentarily across the screen of my memory: "REGION CHAMPIONS" was printed on the back of each shirt and given out each year. The very first year the slogan was "W. A. R.," which stood for "Weights, Attitude and Revenge."

He took a large swallow of water. "The third ingredient is the Community; which includes parents, boosters and local businesses.

Parents and the Booster Club need to be involved on a day-to-day basis. There are many activities for them to get involved in, including working at the snack bar on game days and selling ads for the game program."

"That program's awesome," I told him, "over 60 pages...it's larger than most small college programs and sure got the business community behind the team."

His eyes narrowed slightly again. "If a coach can get parents to focus on the entire football agenda–not just their own son alone– they will have fun working together. When they feel an owner- ship in the program...just like the players must feel an ownership...then they tend to not be critical of it. They will find themselves working for a common cause and develop a camara- derie over the years their son participates."

"I believe that wholeheartedly," I told him.

He stood and got ready to leave the room. "If any of those three groups drops the ball, you'll end up with a fumbled pro- gram."

I sat alone now in the room. Ron's words had left an impact, but even with the clarity of knowing to what he attributed the team's success, I couldn't seem to shake off a feeling of sadness which followed me like a shadow.

It was losing the comradeship of the seniors, that touched some deep chord in me. As Ryan Cobb had poignantly summed it up, in a few sparse words, "It's over," he had said. I wondered if all coaches had the torn remnant of such a sense of loss at the end of a special season. It was hard to let go of such a unique group of young men.

As I was trying to get a pulse on my feelings, I remembered a poem I had heard in the past, entitled "The Ship." The writer was anonymous. Actually the reading was at the funeral of a friend. Strange I should think of it now, but as my mind sifted through the recollection, I realized the message pertained.

As the ship sailed off with the departing people aboard, those left on the shore waved, shouting sadly,"goodbye, goodbye." Then my memory served up the rest of the poem. That same ship would soon be approaching a distant shore, where the people stood on land, happily shouting "hello, hello."

I took comfort in the fact that as our young men left school, embarking on the sea of life, there would be those eagerly waiting to welcome them to the next first down in their lives. Remembering the poem helped to put proper closure to releasing them.

• • •

The first week in April, 1998 I walked into Dana Zupke's sixth period weight training class. John Hogue and Scott Lane were working out. They called out, "Coach Mott–ley," in singsong voices, just the way that Larry Zak and Matt Willden had done. It was like an echo from the past.

Some things never change...

APPENDIX I

The off-season work on weight training and conditioning had paid off, and it showed in the final record of 12 and 1. There was good team depth, good team speed, especially on defense and with the running backs, three of whom ran a 4.5 40 yard dash. And there was good leadership, a good senior class, and the coaches had taken the defense to another level in their design, techniques and strategy. But what really was the difference in this '97 team and the '96 team, which went 5 and 5?

One thing that didn't change was the total offense yardage. In '96 the average total offensive yards per game (YPG) was 394 and in '97 it was 400 YPG. But those yards were arrived at a little bit differently. In '96 the offense rushed for 246 YPG and passed for 148 YPG, while in '97 the offense rushed for 300 YPG and passed for only 100 YPG.

The first downs were about the same: 14 for both '96 and '97; the average yards per rush was close, 6.6 yards per rush in '96, compared to 7.2 yards per rush in '97. The only major difference was in the offensive plays per game. In '96, the offense averaged 53 plays per game, while the opponents only averaged 40 offensive plays per game, which meant that Chaparral had the ball for 13 more plays on average per game than their opponents.

And Chaparral actually had more offensive plays per game in '96 - 55.7, than in '97. The difference was the defense which limited their opponents to 54.3 in '96 and then to only 40 in '97, a drop of 14 plays per game.

The Chaparral defense had made a dramatic turnaround from '96. In 1996 the defense gave up a total of 308 yards per game (YPG) and 198 yards rushing (YPG). In 1997 the defense allowed only 237 YPG and 121 yards rushing per game. The average yards rushing per attempt dropped from 5.2 yards per attempt in '96 to 3.8 yards in '97. The passing yards for opponents was about the same–110 yards per game in '96, and 115 yards per game in '97.

The points allowed by the defense also dropped from 23.5 in '96 to 17 points per game in '97. But the most dramatic turn-around came in the turnovers created by the defense. In '96, Chaparral forced only 11 fumbles and 4 interceptions for a total of 15. In '97, Chaparral forced its opponents into 22 fumbles and 11 interceptions for a total of 33 turnovers by its opponents, including 4 touchdowns by the defense.

In contrast, Chaparral had only 10 turnovers in '97, 7 fumbles and 3 interceptions. In '96 the offense had 24 turnovers, 9 interceptions and 15 fumbles, so the offense had shown dramatic improvement. The bottom line was a *plus 23* in the turnover column, which statistically would put it in the top college and pro teams. In 1996, Chaparral was a minus 9 in the turnover column. So, in the two seasons, it was a turnaround of 32 in turnovers, the most dramatic statistic of the '97 season.

There was one other very positive statistic that showed up in the post-season analysis, and that was the special teams' goals of averaging two times per game of scoring a touchdown or giving the ball to the offense inside the other team's 30 yard line. The special teams did not reach that goal, but it did give the ball to the offense 15 times, and allowed its opponents to only do it 2 times, a difference of 13.

That was a dramatic increase over '96 when the special teams gave up 6 and had only 12 (a difference of 6). Included in the 15 for '97 were four special team touchdowns and two blocked field goals. The punt block team did an outstanding job. They forced a total of 18 times that the opponents' punter had his punts either blocked, forced to run (called a trap) or was rushed so hard that he shanked the punt (any punt that goes under 20 yards). By contrast, Chaparral had no blocks, no traps, and only 3 shanks.

And arguably, the most important statistic–Chaparral was ranked first in the State 4A at the end of the season in power points which reflected its tough schedule. Five of its opponents made the playoffs, but the most dramatic statistical turnaround of 32 turnovers (plus 23 in '97 and minus 9 in '96) can best be summed up by Coach Estabrook's comments:

"In the past, Chaparral had the reputation of being soft–not very physical, and I think that both the players and the coaches wanted badly to turn that around. We wanted to have a team that was physically intimidating–to show no mercy, to be relentless. And when I say 'no mercy', I mean that we would not let up at any time during the game, and all sides of the ball, offense, defense and special teams would have the attitude of delivering a blow first. We wanted our running backs to drop their shoulders when they were being tackled and deliver the blow. It was a mental attitude that the coaches taught and the kids bought into and executed. That attitude caused things to happen, and that's why there was such a dramatic turnaround in turnovers."

APPENDIX II

33   BELLY - Wing Right

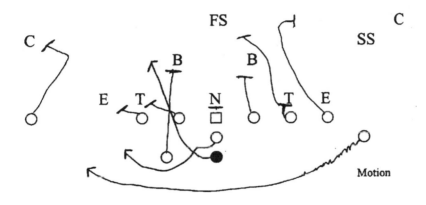

34   BELLY - Slot Left

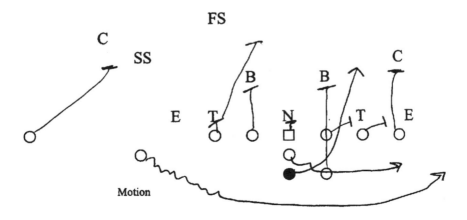

24   COUNTER - Wing Right

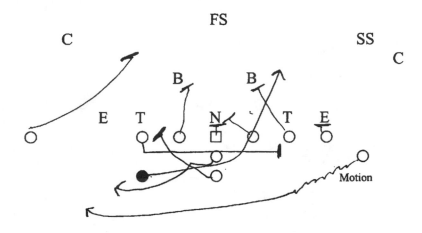

43   COUNTER - Slot Left

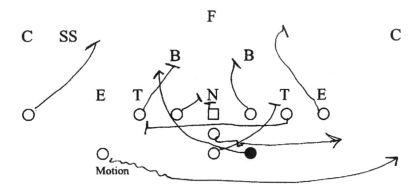

28 SWEEP - Wing Right

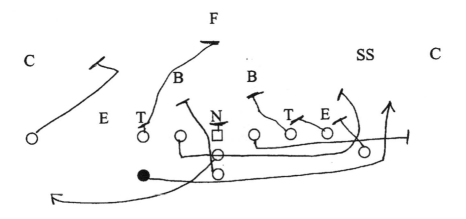

47 SWEEP - Slot Left

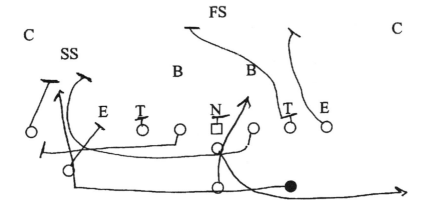

215

32   TRAP - Wing Right

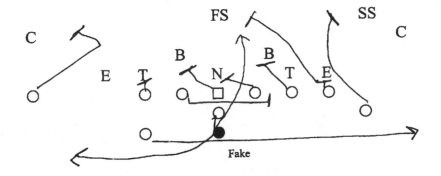

Fake

31   TRAP - Slot Left

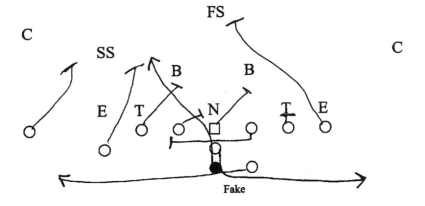

Fake

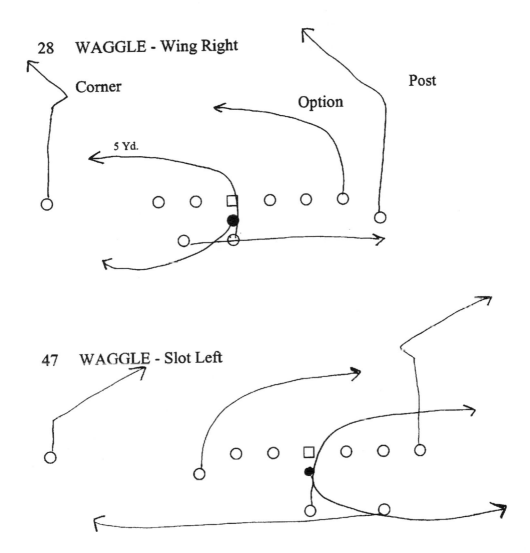

28   WAGGLE - Wing Right

Corner

Option

Post

5 Yd.

47   WAGGLE - Slot Left

SAGUARO - Unbalanced Slot Right

5 yd. Split

○　○　□　○　○　○　　　○
　　　　○　　　　　　○
　　　　○
　　　　○

- Unbalanced Slot Left

○　　○　○　○　□　○　○
　○　　　　　　○
　　　　　　　　○
　　　　　　　　○

NOGALES GAME

33   BELLY PASS - (To Hogue)

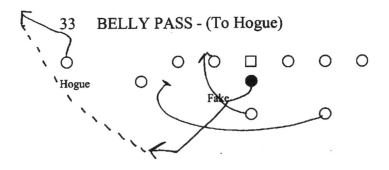

44   BLAST PASS - (To Schwartzberg)

3. ACE

4. TRIPS - Red

LH   RH   TE   SE

TRIPS - Blue

SE   TE   LH   RH

5. DOUBLE TIGHT

FORMATIONS

1.   **WING - Right**

○   ○   ○   □   ○   ○   ○

                          ○   ○

             ○   ○

WING - Left

          ○   ○   ○   □   ○   ○   ○

    ○   ○

                      ○   ○

2.   **SLOT - Right**

○   ○   ○   □   ○   ○   ○

                 ○   ○

       ○   ○

SLOT - Left

○   ○   ○   □   ○   ○   ○

    ○   ○

             ○   ○

SPECIAL TEAMS GAME CHART

CHAPARRAL PUNT OR KICK	YARD LINE KICKED FROM	YARD LINE KICKED TO	HARD LINE RETURNED TO	NET YARDS	HANG TIME	COMMENTS	OPPONENTS PUNT OR KICK	YARD LINE KICKED FROM	YARD LINE KICKED TO	YARD LINE RETURNED TO	NET YARDS

THE TURNAROUND

Hardcover $24.95   _____

Softcover $19.95   _____

    20 or more copies - 50% discount

Shipping & handling add $4.00   _____

For two or more books add
$1.50 each additional book   _____

           TOTAL   _____

TO ORDER BY VISA, MASTERCARD OR
AMERICAN EXPRESS CALL 1-888-265-2732

MAIL <u>COPY</u> OF THIS COUPON WITH CHECK

Jubilee Publishing, Inc.
15560 N. FLW Blvd., B4
PMB #443
Scottsdale, AZ 85260

For questions, please call toll free:
1-877-455-1249

Name: _____

Address: _____

city: _____

Sate: _____   Zip: _____